WALL STREET

Seduction

And Beyond

Renard Johnson

Torquan Publishing
California

WALL STREET SEDUCTION AND BEYOND

Torquan Publishing
California

www.wallstreetseduction.com

Layout and Editing
by Word for Word Editorial
Livermore, California

ISBN 978-0-6155066-3-0
PRINTED IN THE UNITED STATES OF AMERICA

DEDICATION

Sending out love to my charming wife
Lori Moitie', our children Starrlett
and Rejo, family, friends, and
all living creatures.

ACKNOWLEDGMENTS

In writing this book, I became frightened when I was introduced to a derivative beast that was breaking new ground on Wall Street. I'm speaking of no less than the infamous credit default swaps, the financial instrument that would bring the commercial world down to the ground. There is no way I could have done the rudimentary research necessary to illustrate the oncoming monetary pain without my wife Lori's understanding. She didn't quite realize what I was trying to accomplish, but she let me go my own way, and eventually I developed a sketch of a portrait that would turn into this book.

There are also many informed financial wizards on the Internet whom I followed over the years who gave me the straight lowdown on what was happening on the scene. They are too numerous to name all of them. I will name a few who helped me get through the day. Their articles and stock market charts were a part of my therapy. This helped me a great deal back in 2007 and 2008. I thought I was going bonkers following this mess. Their work proved that I was not.

Here's my mini list, not in any special order. Thank you to Mike Whitney, John Brown, Louise Yamada, Mish Shedlock, Robert Shiller, Mike Panzner, Alex Jones, Nouriel Roubini, Elizabeth MacDonald, Jim Rogers, Ron Paul, Doug Kass, Meredith Whitney, Peter Schiff, Marc Faber,

Richard (Mogambo) Daughty, and last but certainly not least is Gerald Celente, founder and Director of The Trends Research Institute.

These brains of the market were right about their claims of a fundamental financial breakdown approaching. Thank you for your service for humanity.

DISCLAIMER

Renard Johnson has never worked nor given any professional advice on investing in the stock market before. The information in this book is not an accusation of a crime by any person or business entity. This author is simply expressing his opinion of an event that is currently developing. Time will be the best judge of just what or who mismanaged the economy into this path of monetary and fiscal downfall.

CONTENTS

I.	The Golden Garbage	1
II.	Good, Decent, Dishonest People	25
III.	Wall Street Meets the Ghetto	45
IV.	The Greatest Story Never Spoken	71
V.	New World Farters … I Mean, Order	89
VI.	The Green Plague	125
VII.	It Still Just Can't Be Called A Crisis	135
VIII.	Sleeping Giants Have Awakened	165
IX.	Plan B	199
About the Author		243

I
The Golden Garbage

THERE I WAS, living what I perceived as a life of joy, trial, and error, just like most people do. At the time, I was working as part of a musical duo along with my wife, Lori, performing for families and kids for many years. This has brought me great joy and satisfaction in my life. Also, I have always kept my eyes on the important events of the day. So, I hawked up my attention to a wicked manipulation of the stock market system. A barrage of government and financial illusions were headed our way. Even as the fiscal times seemed quiet, the monetary world was getting prepared for a major golden goose drop of golden garbage. America's fortune was about to be DOA: dead on arrival.

There are many paths to describe how we got to this forbidden territory. A world living beyond their means. Wall Street multinational corporations, the Federal Reserve, governments, states, counties, cities, and more all saw the light at the end of the get-rich-quick money tunnel that invited them in for cash, jewels, and toxic derivatives tea. Little did the tricksters know that they had just signed Wall Street's death warrant. Most of the unaware public had no clue that the dreams that these scammers were offering were totally unsustainable nightmares from the moment we went to sleep. I tried to get a piece of the golden dream—it turned into a massive case of nervous night sweats. Almost everyone wanted the good life: plenty of money in your bank account, the spacious three-car garage, and a profile of wealth. It seemed too good to be true, but not if you lived in the bubble capital of the world, California. Oh, it was too good to be true. It's the same old story. Financial greed will always cause others to bleed. Balance, people, balance. Not too heavy, too fast.

While working through the process of penning this life record of my economic experiences, I titled this book *Wall Street Seduction and Beyond.* I originally started with the intention of sticking to more or less a stock market crash theme, but there was no way that I could omit the rest of this epic saga which also concerns politics and war. You can't separate politics from finance. They go hand in glove ... especially the politicians and Wall Street. The complexities of the world's financial pitfalls are all tightly woven into a nanoknot of intricacy between finance, war, and life itself. You know, money affects living and life affects money. So this is a book about my panoramic journey of viewing the financial events that we are uncovering in our lives today, which go on to cause our troubles. I'm also writing about the economic and political mistakes of the past and their lasting effects on future generations. Man's foolish lust for wealth and power is driving this carriage right over the cliff.

To start this off with a bang, in the autumn of 2008 some politicians and Wall Streeters thought for sure that the global economic market collapse was imminent. This was the End! There was a grand shaking at the foundation of finance—worldwide! I went through this momentous episode play by play. I rode the wave of financial insanity.

I saw the wave coming from the years before. I knew that this was a real homeland insecurity threat, and not just some figment of someone's imagination, not only to America but to the entire world at large. Really scary if you were there. It was super-colossal. I still have problems breathing when I reflect on these times. I kept asking myself, how did we get this close to obliteration? These times made Hurricane Katrina look like a walk in the park—no disrespect to the good folks of my home state of Louisiana. If nothing else, the establishment scared the world and the world didn't know it. I knew these folks' hearts were beating fast; they were aware of this. I feel that just because I caught that rogue wave of delirium, I get to write about it. I'll have more to say about the collapse later.

I wouldn't care if King Kong himself was elected president of the nation over the last decade: If he left this massive of a mess, then he should be a part of the financial conversation that would cause citizens to disapprove of his money management methods, to say the least. Let me state that just recently in December 2009 while I was in the process of wrapping up this book, the *Wall Street Journal* published an article reviewing the last decade from an economic standpoint, entitled, "The Lost Decade." It validated everything that I had already written in this book as far as the severity of the situation. I had an idea that this was a big economic deal. This article screamed the facts—1999 to 2009 was the worst decade for the U.S. stock market since record keeping began in the 1820s. This means that was the worst stock market calendar decade in America's history. The decade of zero gains. Sub zero gains. This explains the pain the public at home and away are experiencing today. You just can't get any worse than the generation that holds this dubious honor.

I keep telling people this is an actual event that will have major repercussions for years to come. The U.S. administration and congress in charge during this time period must be just dripping with pride, knowing that they dropped an "F bomb" (F for financial) and blew up the stock exchange. As a matter of fact, I believe that all local, state, national, and international politicians should claim full responsibility for the quaking of the financial homeland insecurity. Where were they?

Let's go way back through the halls of time. Remember the years of the New Millennium? Who were the president and his posse during the worst years in the stock market's history? Can you say the George W. Bush administration? Who? Don't take my word for this fact. Just Google, Bush lost decade and nose around. The point is that Bush/Cheney and the entire political system, along with the Wall Streeters, have disintegrated the economic fundamentals of the free market capitalistic business model. Their non-leadership bled the nation-state dry. They created a deficit of over four trillion dollars and counting in just eight short years... and that's a conservative number just for the Neo Conservatives. Thank you very much!

All the deficits of the previous presidents combined could not begin to compare to this debt bomb. A more accurate description would be to call it a mirage of money management. It was the reversal of prudent observation and regulation. These people must have assumed that they were voted into power to deregulate the entire world. Wall Street wiped out over eight trillion dollars off of the stock market books in 2008 alone. Seems like a long time ago. Not to me.

A pattern of monetary maliciousness infested the market. A Washington-Wall Street head-on collision screamed toward us. The nosedive that this nation and the world experienced is unparalleled in terms of degree, yet still, not much notice of these horrific facts seems to be pressworthy. Even though peoples' troubles are tied directly to this event of uncharted greenback failure, they are still hard pressed to understand what's happening to them. Hence this book. I've decoded a small part of the puzzle about the largest dollar slamdown in the United States' history. As I always stress: Take everything in this book with a grain of salt. Use it as a guide to do your own research. It's just fascinating to me, not being a financial expert, that I zoomed in on this mammoth market disruption when many experts didn't see it coming.

I also had this baffling theory: If the stock market of the last ten years that we just experienced was the worst decade ever, even more down than the 1930s Depression, then could we be in a depression not spoken about? Just a mind worm. My final hit on this topic is that both political parties were in charge during this decade of delusion. Yet, they are afraid to shine a light on the fact that their parties were leading the way when the lowest returns from the stock market ever happened. This was on their watch. These people wanted to make history. Well, they did. Every day is historically important now. There are record budget deficits breaking the public's bank accounts. Furthermore, the cities, counties, states, and nations all around the world are observing many significant financial firsts. I hope everyone understands that there are consequences for the most pitiful stock market performance that the world has just witnessed. There's a reason for the seductive season. "Show me the money!"

The Wealth Creation

This is not a book about the economic theory of analyzing charts from the computerized minds of newly minted economic postgraduate students or old stock market pros. The adventure you're about to embark on is the result of my personal addiction to a financial phenomenon that will be one day known as a legendary economic tsunami. I'm speaking about the infamous credit crunch. As I wrote in the introduction, I became aware of the impending economic shakedown a few years ago, when there were hardly any articles on the Internet about the troubles that would lie ahead.

Being a common man without a broad awareness of the everyday workings of Wall Street, I took on the challenge of decoding all the lingo, and to my surprise, I found that the people on Wall Street didn't know what the hell was going on, either. That's obvious by the financial gambling that was turned loose on the stock market lending packages. The underhanded dealing of cards that were falling from the bottom of their economic decks was full of phony bank credit default swaps. These exotic swap instruments were the slickest financial garbage the world has ever seen. The derivatives plan devised by these lawyers, lobbyists,

Wall Street types, and politicians confused the market to perfection. I remember studying these instruments of mass destruction, and all I saw was a con game. As I became engrossed in the mechanics of this fake paper in the fall of 2006, I began to see a vision of what was to come. Something very ugly was heading our way. Something unstoppable.

Now, it's a new decade, and to speak about the economic blowup in connection to the Bush administration is nearly forbidden. Hell, that was eight years of pain that we are still paying for. These people were not in charge of some small-time prom chaperon job. I am complaining no less about the current conditions left by these chaperons of the free-market capital enterprise system. These were mind-blowing times of fiscal "loosey-goosey."

The question that came to mind was, were we really that weak in leadership? These people are too old to be half that delusional, but they were. That answers that. You can always use this book as a fire starter in your chimney. You may think I made up this whole book out of the blue, but that's not the case. Look around at the financial landscape. Something is going down. I don't know everything and never claimed to know everything, but I do know this: The world is about to reach an economic boiling point. Just because certain folks want to have amnesia, that doesn't mean everyone has to. They need to stop these head games.

If we could just recover the trillions that the politicians squandered, we could save America's economy—and the world's—today! Now, this is an act that would really make

America, and the planet, safer for real. Not just some lip service from lost souls.

You Know Who

Sometimes it's just easier to focus on the Bush administration than the Wall Street CEOs because their faces were more known, and it's not like you had to go around making stories up on these characters. They provided the inquiring minds with all the ammo we needed. Always putting their feet in their mouths. Most people don't know the Wall Street bunch as well as they know the politicians. Let's name a few stock exchange legends anyway. Jamie Dimon, chairman of JPMorgan; Kenneth D. Lewis, formerly CEO and Chairman of Bank of America; Vikram Pandit of Citigroup, and so on. It would take a lot more time and reserves to chase down these guys' stories during the crunch than I have to give. I did see them perform live and in color on TV and the Internet. You can still find them on YouTube from back in the day if you're willing to do a little research. Obviously, these guys missed the call.

They have a phrase on Wall Street. The media asks the experts, "What is the market telling you today?" I guess these knowledgeable ones were not listening in class very well. How could they have missed this market call of unprecedented imperfections when they were there daily? That's why they missed it, in my opinion. You had to be outside of Wall Street's reach to scope this one-of-a-kind event out. A guy like me had a better chance of making the call if I did the work to discover this commercial neglect. The economy has been walking on cripple for decades, but the Bush/Cheney administration skyrocketed our debt allowance to new record levels. This is the gorilla in the cabinet that no one wants to let out. I don't care what their names are; when some suckers drop a four to five trillion dollar tab on your nation and tells the public, "Nice knowing you," you call them what they are: major screwups! Perhaps they had fun. We sure are not!

Method to the Madness

So, there I was in the fall of 2006, researching the economic happenings daily, eight to twelve hours a day—totally involved in the Internet and the crony TV shows, trying to get every kernel of valuable data about the coming economic drop off. I was committed to making sense out of this madness, if I could. My wife thought I was going nuts. I was sure I was going nuts. I was going wacky. How could you not go insane following this deception of biblical proportions? There I was, learning about stuff I didn't even know existed until then. I'm talking about the parallel dimensions of money.

To put it bluntly, there's one money market for the commoners and a hidden crime money scam for the elites. The hedge fund instruments are also the greatest garbage game being played in the market, but they serve a necessary purpose in balancing the market. So how could I not lose my mind, especially when not a lot of people didn't recognize the oncoming mistakes (to put it mildly), of Wall Street and the spineless "Washington Yellow House"? This was a fine quantum exhibit of corrupt money entanglement. I realized the mission I was on is the equivalent of climbing an economic Mount Everest. I'd have a better chance of flying on the back of that golden goose of Wall Street than interpreting this stock stuff.

Sometime I would stare into the computer in disbelief at what I just read or heard. At this time, I'm starting to notice a major disconnect between the major news channels and the real reporting of what's happening as the credit crunch approach. There's no one I could really talk to about this, because pretty much everyone else was so far behind the curve, especially Wall Street, Main Street, and Washington. It's a terrifying situation.

Remember, this is going on toward the end of 2006 into 2007. By now, those who are meant to know are reading the writing on the wall and it spells out the phrase "Holy shit." What's even scarier is that the leaders had no clue during this time, including the Federal Reserve. They ran a very fiscally conservative budget. Not! Let's get for real; they still have no clue today. But that's an event within itself that I'll cover in a later chapter.

Wall of Worry

So, the spring of 2007 is here and nothing is turning out right. The currency current is going in the wrong direction, and the case for Americans' financial security is evaporating extremely quickly. By this time, I'm running around hardly sleeping, and pacing the floor when I'm awake, feeling that something "gihugic" is going down, but not knowing exactly what. Hey, I'm trying to understand an event that has never happened before in this country, or in this world for that matter. So it ain't easy trying to figure this out, even with the multiple hours of daily research that I was engulfed in. There was no map to follow. Then the summer of 2007 hit, and that's when one of the greatest financial crackups of all time happened. The infamous "credit crunch" broke out. This was also seen as the day the bottom fell out of Wall Street, for those who were paying attention. It was ugly before the crunch, but when that spectacle went down, those who had been following the story with devotion also died some that summer. I lost my way and became dazed and baffled. All this time I'm still performing for crowds, smiling on the outside, sometimes confused on the inside. Talk about the horror of money meteors dismantling the global financial grid. The credit crunch was all of that and more!

That's about the size of it. It was one of the saddest things I've ever seen. Still, when I look back on those times, I know they are directly tied to the pain we are experiencing today. Most people don't really understand to this day how relevant this event was in their life of wealth and safety. I cried when this happened. I knew that America and the world had lost something that we would never be able to regain again. So far, we haven't. We lost the trust and certainty of the markets from the retail investors' perspective. The little investor that could really is the tail that wags the Wall Street dog.

Economic Storyteller

From then on, all bets were off. The floodgates opened, and a deluge of bad news hit Wall Street. Talk about running like chickens with their heads cut off! The race was on to see who could get to the failing subsidized option ARM loans exits first. Countrywide Home Loans was reeling backwards. The home loan lending industry soon became a graveyard of refinancing dreams turned into bankrupt nightmares. One important fact is that no one informed the people about the latest monetary emergencies. To recognize the circumstances of the shakeout, you had to have been not just following the economic slamdown, but you would have to know your purpose for your devotion to this event. It ain't for the weak of heart to have grinded it out with this metric magic money machine called Wall Street. I felt helpless. I am nobody to listen to about your financial world. I have no professional experience. Who would listen to me? So I sit in my awareness of the grief that was about to roar down on the folks who had no clue what is a credit crunch and its importance to all the folks' lives, whether they're in the stock market or not.

At that moment, I realized a new position in the world was required: an economic storyteller. Someone who had a grand overview of what was going down at warp speed, at the same time knowing I had to evaluate how this deflating system would affect my family and me. So, there I was stuck in the middle. On one side, I was totally concerned for the world's economic downfall, but at the same time I still had to keep an eye out for what's critical to me and my family's happiness. I knew one thing for sure. Either way it was going to be ugly. A hard-to-win situation. We all lost something on this corporate gamble.

I came to the deduction that if I was going to be inconvenienced by internal systematic enemy pressures of the financial and political nature, I might as well know who's bringing the agitation and from where. There would be days when I would sometimes kick this economic subject around with my cousin, Lemoine Turner. A few of years ago, I told him that the "Bush-crap" of budget neglect was about to hit the fan. Hence, this is my journey of how I started looking for the economic boogie man.

It began many moons ago. One of my first wishes was to try to have enough information so I could inform others that something big is happening, and that we needed to pay attention. But what would it look like? I'm talking a major disruption on Wall Street. What would it feel, sound, and smell like? So, I dove in soul first. I knew my spirit was up to the challenge of developing the tenacious altitude that would be necessary to ride the rogue wave of this ominous situation. This was no small feat. A funny thing about this metro event. I kept telling Lori that I wished something really significant had caused this shakeup. Not just a lack of leadership, stupidity, blindness, non-governmental regulatory controls, greed, plus a lot of other bonehead techniques. I became frightened and downright scared for two reasons. One reason was that the media was in the blind and had no clue what all this meant, so they could not inform the public correctly.

Second, I had a feeling that I had opened the bad genie bottle, and I didn't comprehend all the complications and ramifications that came with this territory. Somebody had to tell this story so the average person could understand what happened. There were only a few calling the shots straight, and even if you listened to them at that time, no one could interpret what they were saying. So I bided my time and kept researching and digging into the ocean of garbage numbers, trying to get what this all meant. Just to think, here I am a newbie at this whole game, and I am doing this for my family and the world. Going off half-cocked, attempting to ride the economic rogue wave of the century. Ain't nothing like diving in head first. So, I dove into the quicksand of the quotas again.

The Financial Gain of Pain

Many days, my brain would literally hurt from the exhaustion of reading dozens of articles, trying to get a handle on this once-in-a-lifetime event. I promised myself I would hang in there even when I wanted nothing to do with this crap. Some days I would say to myself, the hell with this crap, I can't follow it anymore. Then I would come across a story of concern and dive right back into the crazy mix of delusions.

My music job has always been my therapy of playing music for happy folks. Thank my lucky stars for that. Entertaining for families made my life worth living. When the credit crunch happened, I had already put in a year and a half of studying the market daily. I was getting physically and mentally worn out. By this time, I was taking a lot of body blows. But I knew I had to gut this mission out that I had brought on myself. I didn't won't anyone to tell me how the story went and how we got into this whale of a mess. So I hung in there, mostly for myself and mainly for the people. I knew the politicians would miss this whole chapter in America's history. Once again, the credit crunch was expected by me and others, but no one would listen. When that bitch of a credit bang blew up, most media and others kept saying the old phrase, "This too shall pass." Guess what? Four years and counting for me, it's still here.

Well, my collected knowledge by now knew we were headed for the point of no return, if we didn't get wiser people at the controls and fast! None of the smart people were allowed positions of power that had enough free market awareness to salvage the stock market. So the smart financial folks had to continue to spread the word through the Internet. The whole financial media contest had transformed the credit crash into a politicized mantra of "Relax, everything is under control."

I felt so sad for the people and animals because I saw a disconnect from reality by the economic reporters, the media and the actual events. There was no turning back. The bottom was not only falling out, but now I could see right down to the black hole of the financial core. The Hellhole of Wall Street. It is bleeding profusely. Blood on the hands of so many wicked-intentioned souls gone bad. There's blood on Wall Street's stock exchange floor and it's deepening daily. Somebody call that $400K-a-year janitor to clean it up and dispose of the goods, which are the bads.

I became depressed from time to time, and some days were better than others. I had no one to talk to about this in 2007. No one wanted to hear this downer yak-yak. So there I was all alone, watching the walls of the American empire crumble like Atlantis. Inside, I was screaming out to all who would listen and there were not many. You must remember that the real estate boom was still in full effect in 2007. Most people were under the impression that their wealth was safe and secure. Outside of me, I was silent as a mouse, trying not to annoy people who were years behind on this story. I knew that they had a great chance of never recovering from this breakdown of financial non-ethics. Often I would question myself, why was I crazy enough to dive into this slimefest? I must have been out of my mind, but then again for those who didn't jump into the economic junkyard because of time restraints or whatever, they might eventually lose their material possessions along with their sanity. So I kept chugging alone into the abyss of emptiness, not so much hoping for miracles but lost, looking for something but not knowing what. It was a lonely route of doubt as the market kept getting worse.

Then I started to depend on my philosophical background to get me through this cave of despair. I have always followed the wisdom path that there are universal laws that are eternal and cannot be broken by mankind. I also know manmade laws are temporary and are constantly changing. Then I had an epiphany in my feeble mind and started to ask the question, what if women controlled the system of finance? Would we still have the lack of oversight, outrageous greed and selfishness that is wreaking havoc on the wealth of the world today, caused mostly by men who violated manmade laws? Probably not. Then are the universal laws being challenged by these weak-of-heart male scammers? (Of course they are!)

For example, one universal law is nothing in excess, everything in moderation. In other words, beware of greed. Well, you would have to be a fool to dispute this law, and there were many fools who lost their moral compass chasing the loot. People in finance and politics who were fitting the truth to the shape of their heart. The train wreck that we are witnessing today is a direct result of the breaking of this law. Even though mankind breaks his laws all the time, no one gets to break the universal laws and get away with it.

The credit crunch is proof of this. A foreclosure epidemic that began in late 2006 in the U.S. continues to drain wealth from consumers and erodes the financial strength of banking institutions. Look around at the financial landscape today, and you'll see suffering everywhere you look, not exclusively caused by the subprime slime loans. By now, I am used to the thought of wealth hemorrhaging, even though I reject the idea that the credit crunch could not have been avoided.

Here's a novel theory. Symbolically speaking, maybe the stock market economy is really an energetic female entity with males in charge. Therefore, that could be causing the conflicts. It's a woman's world. The male-dominated society way of being is finished. So, now we all must pay for the ignorance of the few men. Isn't that the way the story goes from long ago? The underdogs must pay for the mistakes of the top dogs? When we bail out the economic system as taxpayers, we are assisting in a federal and global economic health plan that keeps this failed system on life support by giving green money to fill those corporate oxygen tanks.

A Long Time to End an Empire

The anguish I felt during the credit crunch, and still do feel daily, is one of great disillusions and disappointments affecting all mankind. This did not have to be! This shift of legal tender exploitation would eventually take the entire planet out of focus. There were some days in the summer of 2007 that I thought the world could just end any day. Here we are, just a few years later, and I should have known that it takes a long time to build an empire and a long time to end an empire. It was a feeding frenzy when the crunch happened.

On the days the stock market tanked, many thought it would never return to a decent level. It was so erratic that the day after a tumble, the market would regain nearly all of the previous day's losses. It was wacked. It still is. People's lives depended on the market tendencies, as some followed it closely with great intensity and others just assumed the stock market would always come back. By this time I was preparing for the worst. In early 2008 I got out of the market completely and told everybody I knew to do so, but not many people listened to me. That's understandable because I was ahead of the curve.

The credit market got so tight that it actually dematerialized from its previous form to some kind of obscure, obtuse, invalid imposter of a stock exchange. What's new about that? Absolutely nothing! It's just that now, millions of citizens have given their life savings and pensions to the buzz saw called Wall Street, and the returns did not materialize. As a matter of fact, in my humble opinion, this along with other pressures of life, such as living in a country with layers upon layers of taxes, fees, and time- and wealth-draining regulations, are brain-draining the citizenry. I wouldn't be surprised if most Americans suffer from WWSPTSD: Washington/Wall Street Post-Traumatic Stress Syndrome. I know I'm worn out. What about you?

These disasters not only through our lives into instant imbalance, but in some ways the whole system of finance that's interlinked with the human mind also becomes disoriented. We were trained all of our lives in America to grow up and become rich and successful. Maybe I can go so far as to say we are mentally integrated with our currency procedures, even though they are ill-conceived operations. Our consciousness is directly affected by the actions of the stock market, and the market is also affected by human thinking. We are entangled with the stock market whether you want be or not. Just look at all the people who were not even involved with Wall Street who are still getting burned by the dysfunction of the dicey action from the blind monetary visionaries.

When Lehman Bros. collapsed in October 2008, the financial foundation of the entire world shook as it never had before. A financial nuke blew up in the face of the nation and the world on the Bush administration's watch. Neither Cheney nor Bush could see that the flood gates of global economic change were upon them, us, and the world: Not just the commerce companies, but all companies and humanity lost something that day. What we lost is difficult to comprehend. We lost prestige in the eyes of all those who had belief in America's ability to be a responsible financial citizen of the world community. Many have sacrificed their lives before us to give us the opportunity of integrity, freedom, and basic human and monetary protections against corrupt systems of racketeering. Governments must never compromise the right of every person to live their lives as their Creator sees fit. That's just part of what we lost.

In the last few years, the world has experienced the ten greatest bankruptcies in modern man's history. America has become the poster child for being a banana republic. Still, we are counting more and more corporations falling off the cliff monthly. This is in large part the effect of the impact of the credit crunch front and center. The game of "extend and pretend" is headed for a collision with austerity plans for the nation. Is America's resolve too weak to reduce its debt? That's the question. Ain't no rainbow at the end of these failed financial contracts. What is "Obama Custer" going to do now? You could use the Western vernacular: "Look, General Obama, them austerity Indians done circle back behind us, Obama, sir. They coming up from the rear and the sides at lightning speed. What's next, General? Call Texas and ask Bush. He helped start these fires."

Maintain in the Insane

While living with the markets from the beginning of the collapse, trying to keep any level of sanity was demanding. My determination was like the song: "I'm still standing." I lived to tell about it—that's the difference between this author and others who released new books on the state of the economy. On this particular event of the credit crunch and the crash of 2008, I was totally engaged with the oncoming train wreck from the beginning. I had even connected the futuristic dots to where this event had to happen. It could not be avoided and it was not avoided. When many other prognosticators went to their daily jobs and missed the calls of the markets, each day I spent many hours researching the corruptive force called Wall Street and Washington politics from multiple angles. During the early days, finger pointing and blame for this debacle was a common conversation. I have seen many articles blaming the Bush administration, as well as the former and current Wall Street head "corpo-cronies" for letting this discharge of monetary demons loose on the world. When the administration changed, at first there wasn't much in the way of accountability, but lately, there has been more examination of how it all happened.

For me, it became an obsession to chase the truth that never was. The more I checked on the money concerns, the more I realized that it's the same way as it always was. The few at the top of the ladder create the crime, and the unfortunate fools at the bottom of the financial totem pole pay the debt of the crimes. So, what's new? The difference is that more information is available to the masses to become better informed. Shockingly, I have no idea why more people are not diving into this juicy story, and the epic consequences and outcomes that lay ahead. I had to know that if my life would be disrupted, who, what, when, where, and why would be responsible. Thank God for the Internet. I can understand why, and at the same time feel empathy for them. My experience is roughly four and a half years ahead of most people in this game; for the people who are not paying any attention to this epoch, I'm sure it's probably even more.

When I've tried to give folks a heads up on what's up, they will listen but never make a move. In some ways, I don't blame them. I couldn't imagine even starting to try to comprehend what's going on in this economic meat grinder. It would give me a feeling of hopelessness. Even now, with the head start I have, it still gives me that feeling from time to time. That's why I wrote this. I knew something the world had never seen before was approaching, and I didn't want to have to get the true story from anyone else. It's been rough, but one way or another everyone will have to pay for the moral degradation of others.

There are others who were there in the beginning of this fiasco calling it right, too many to name, but I salute these brave men and women for their candor and forthrightness, especially when conventional wisdom told us the housing market would rise, easy credit was there to stay, and that our investments would never really be at risk. It's been a difficult journey in telling part of the story about how the greatest economy and culture in modern times lost its way.

So, you see my friends, sometime economic hunting ain't pretty. As a matter of fact, it's pretty much downright distasteful, especially when you're the hunted like the general public is. The "show me the money" trail is a long and twisting road. No one actually knows exactly where it's going. In this author's view, it looks like a beautiful country road full of green scenery, but which may be leading to a dead end drop-off. Buckle up, because this is going to be the ride of your lifetime, your children's lifetime, and your grandchildren's lifetime, as well. Extreme economic gain brings extreme pain. Let's say it together, class: "Deleveraging! Ain't it fun?"

A Strange Love Story

Strangely, I fell in love with this epic tale of fiscal fractions. How could I not, when I spent more time digging into this cliffhanger than I did eating and sleeping some days. It still blows me away that the mainstream media is not just all over this news maker like green on money. Well, maybe not—the press has been compromised by aligning themselves with the creators of this possible fall of civilization as we know it. They may never get another chance at a saga this impressive ever again.

So, I took on this project as an economic investigator. It chose me, I didn't choose it. I wasn't that interested in this topic until just a few years ago, when I notice a foul odor in the economic air. Now, years later, I'm fairly confident that it was well worth the effort. This knowledge has brought me a feeling of comfort, if that word is the appropriate term to use in this case, about where my life is heading. At least I know a fair amount about this subject and I won't be totally blindsided.

Now, calling that a comfort zone is risky in itself; actually, I am anything but comfortable. My mind is fried from this trail of hell after traveling down the road following this mind-blowing story of extend-and-pretend for a very long time. America has unhinged its doors of hardship and strife, and opened them wide on unsuspecting voting constituents. We can't let humanity become a footnote in the halls of history. We, as a species, still have too much more to accomplish for the better good of all living things in the universe.

If we could just master world peace the way most world leaders ignite world wars, we could easily reverse the negative effects caused by ignorance. We would instantly become a world-class example of right living by having a golden heart, instead of just having a bank account full of golden eggs. We must first realize that our world is so fragile that a single egomaniacal political-financial system of backward visions can cause the elimination of an entire environmental, economic, and public system of life if we are all not careful. This is a strange love story, indeed.

II

Good, Decent, Dishonest People

First, let's get one thing straight right off the top. This financial F-up is a reptile brain event. A linear thinking commotion. This economic crackup is caused exclusively, strictly and totally by mankind's shady, crafty, double-dealing, fraudulent, look-the-other-way sinister motives. This legal tender disappearance of public funds is unfair to say the least, disastrous to say the worst. No civilization should have to go through what we are going through. I heard many people refer to these times as this nation having with Bush fatigue by the time 2008 rolled around, just as we experienced Clinton fatigue in 2000. I could not see Wall Street being a pillar of honor, while the crack house in Washington was open for business. So both operations were snarled in lawlessness, and soon became two extremely disorganized rat dens of financial pandemonium. I am no saint by any means, so as I explain my opening remarks in this chapter, you too might concur that it is an unscrupulous lot who are the principals of these unjust tribulations we all will have to live through. It all comes down to people not keeping their word. Let's talk about the concept of a human being keeping their word.

Your Word is Your Bond

If a person cannot, or will not, honor their word, all is lost anyway. A government's word is all they have to keep any free country from falling into chaos. The word "credit" comes from "credibility," or faith that a person, state, or country will do what they pledge they would do. That credit card application you filled out? The company granting you that line of credit depends on your ability and willingness to pay back the money that you borrowed, fulfilling the terms that you agree to. What kind of chaos would result if we all applied for mortgages, credit cards, and car loans without any intention to keep our promise to repay that note? The worldwide repercussions that resulted from a relatively small percentage of people defaulting on their mortgages are still being strongly felt. It will take years for the worldwide economy to recover from that event.

If a person, state, country or nation does not honor their word, there can be no freedom, no democracy, no justice, and no civilization. The leader who takes the position of power and does not have the dignity to speak the truth has not only harmed themselves but also their country and the world for generations to come. This is why the political representatives who are voted into power take an oath to uphold justice and defend the Constitution. They must not demonstrate that they have had a pretty careless upbringing by not keeping their word.

Without this ethical bond of truth and fairness for all beings receiving respect and being held in high regard, the very people and system of justice that the conductors of the law are supposed to protect and safeguard for the public's benefit is lost. That would unconstitutionally destroy every positive move for self-realization that this and any nation standing for freedom has built in the past and is trying to build on in the future. It's been said that a nation is no stronger than its people. I'd like to add a caveat to that: a nation is no stronger than its people and its leaders.

Some leaders are weak and some are strong, the same as the general public. Leadership is a rare quality, and most are not cut out to wear this badge of honor. Today, we are witnessing many politicians who took the oath of office, and then have fallen into disgrace. The destruction of wealth we are realizing now was created in the minds of men and women. There are many factors behind this breakdown, but one of the main reasons is the moral untrustworthiness of those in authority. Unless the leaders are above board with the masses, the weight of their treachery will destroy everything in sight.

No one is above the law. Where the law only protects a few folks, there is no law. We are a nation of laws, not of men. This is an extremely important rule. The people who are trusted to be in charge of administering the legal process must be constantly doubted, asked about questions or suspicions, aggravated, regulated and flat-out insulted if it's called for. They must never be comfortable with their positions of authority, and it's our obligation as citizens—their bosses—to keep them under our microscope. They answer to us ... not the other way around. That's the main reason that the Founding Fathers wrote the Declaration of Independence and the Constitution: to stop weak leaders in their tracks. It's the very fabric of any just democracy that came before our current civilization, and for those who will be here after us. Without these virtuous, unprejudiced principles of behavior, there can be no such thing as civilization.

In my view, this is the fundamental reason that our financial foundations of trust have been rocked to the core. Unless we right this ship of lawless transgressions, the very future of all human beings is at stake. We are all in the rat hole of finance now. We are going to have to climb out of this bottomless pit ourselves. There are not going to be any miracles.

Public Abandonment

In my opinion, someone has to be cuckoo here. Either it's the creators of the financial doomsday who are ludicrous, or it's the people who were trying to prevent this misfortune. Misinformation experts like Karl Rove and your pick of Wall Street cheerleaders will always try to confuse the issues to save their careers. When we observe the results of their hare-brained actions, any sane person would say that absolutely, these folks are bonkers.

If you let those who had a hand in the breakdown tell the story, then the facts get all twisted, turned around, and they claim that the public brought about their own bad financial luck. These false leaders claim they had no hand in creating this financial catastrophe. The media just goes along for the ride to Miseryland. They are all traveling around the country today, trying to rewrite history to put them in a better light. It won't work!

There's a reason that we are staring into the well of money mistakes. They are directly connected to this precedent of accepting the idea that none of the double crossing, cunning heroes who are really zeroes, are being held accountable for their actions. They took a pledge to uphold, and not break, the law. I don't have a lot of love lost for these hoodwinking villains. Why should you or I have any regard for the bleeders of our funds? After all, the Wall Street Journal stated that we have just gone through the worst financial decade since the creation of this nation. That should be worth a Congressional hearing or two. I'm aware that there was a financial inquiry in February 2010, looking into the financial boom and blow up, but they did not include the administration that had oversight of the nation at that time. These people spent tons of money and lost tons of money. How could you have an all-encompassing inquiry without some of the main culprits involved? This book and others like it may be the only broader inquiry you'll ever get. So, "shut up and keep watching the cuckoo debt clock as your life ticks by!" The ticking is getting louder. Wait a minute. It's not a clock at all, but an economic bomb about to explode! Those guys and their cute hide-the-budget games.

Besides, most of the politicians missed the credit crunch and the recession anyway, so how could they hold an inquiry of the economic facts when they don't really know what happened? If the Financial Commission did know what happened, and this breakdown was either allowed, or done on purpose, then that is an even more deceitful crime. So, what did you know and when did you know it? If you did know and did nothing to stop this, well, the hell with you, too. The honor of mankind's progress is on the line. It's time to step up. The consciousness of humanity is the one gift that belongs to no one person or organization. It belongs to all living souls.

As I write these words, I look at how the monetary system has been bombed by immoral hominid drones capable of wreaking wide paths of destruction on the pocketbook and lifestyles of the many. If they had not abandoned the groundwork laid out in the U.S. Constitution, we would not be in this dire nightmare. Know that everyone's financial rights have been violated not by moral, noble, good, and pure individuals, but rather vile, wicked, and depraved characters who still sleep well at night. Meanwhile, many people stay awake all night, paralyzed with fear gripping their financial souls. These demented non-citizen leaders are still walking around, unaware of the damage they have caused. Their spirits are dark. The despair they have brought upon the planet still goes unchecked. People can get rich destroying a nation the same as building a nation, but destroying a nation is easier.

Higher Educational Degrees

I have always wondered why such stock (pun intended) was put in college educational degrees in this country. Of course, I believe in higher education and believe that every child should have the right to go to a college or university if that is their desire. These days it looks like the dream to earn a degree is becoming a relic of the past. I went to college myself. My point is that the college degree does not make the person. The person makes the degree. There are so many who abused their degrees, and use it for purposes other than for making a contribution to society.

These power mongers take advantage of the connections they can achieve by graduating from certain institutions. It often makes me wonder why someone is revered for having a piece of paper, when at the same time that paper does nothing to clarify the intentions of that person's motives. It's the classic example of looks being deceiving, when you look at the financial ruins of today.

Most of these fiscal geeks have impressive college degrees, but what good are all the fancy accolades if you are not trustworthy graduates? Of course, I'm not saying all of Wall Street is dishonest. There are a lot of good, hard-working, honest folks down in the pit of the stock exchange and offices everywhere: regionally, nationally, and globally. I am criticizing the higher ups who saw what was happening, and did nothing and said nothing. I'm sure if you go into the offices of the top CEOs, you will see the most impressive diplomas your eyes will ever witness. Also the recipient of this award will also let you know in most cases, the proud heritage of his former University or college with great vigor and boast.

That's my point: Who cares about the prestige of that diploma if the person behind that paper does not honor its merit? A higher-level college degree can get you past the gates of inquiry, and let you breeze into the land of the plenty. The only problem is they will take us with them to this hellhole of a major life education. Now we are all on the run from a crash of the educational and economic systems.

Just think, what would happen if most on Wall Street and in Washington politics did not honor their degree's commitment to excellence or their oaths? What kind of world would we have? You would have systemic breakdowns all over the place. You could even call out a warning that we have a failed external control system. It's a good thing that would never happen, right?

Financial Terrorism

I checked Wikipedia and typed in the term "financial terrorism," and came up with a long list of governmental security organizations. I have my own definition of the term: It's when an entire financial system and the government support of that system becomes so interconnected with crony capitalism that their mere corrupt convulsions can cause the whole system to collapse. That's financial terrorism. The folks at the top of the food chain get the rewards, and the people at the bottom pay the bills. That's one of the foundations of fascism and communism. Also, our nation's Treasury is being depleted by the powers to be. How do you like that definition? Sounds like a hit job. A Federal Reserve contract on the public funds from the inside out.

You see, this is the terrorism that I am really concerned with, because it is this path that we are currently on that is capable of ending the dreams of the young and old at a moment's notice. I call it the green plague. Forget about the swine flu. The green plague is planetwide right now, and is causing the death of billions of dollars and Euros in peoples' bank accounts. There are living souls whose hard earned monies are in those bank accounts. The contagion has spread across the planet and devoured trillions of dollars of wealth, bank accounts and never made a sound. A chapter on the Green Plague is coming up in this book.

I'm not worried about the terrorist with the ammunition and roadside bombs, although these are atrocities themselves. The way I see it, the bombers usually kill or injure less than five hundred victims at a time, 9/11 being a horrendous exception. I am not excusing these people who commit these unforgiveable crimes against humanity. They will have to stand before their creator and ask forgiveness to cover their soul's crimes. I'm more horrified by the silent assassins, with the firepower of the presidential and congressional pen that never makes a sound. They have the terror weapons of power to create a planet of suffering.

Take a peek at what's going on today with the money game. This ain't no small-time terrorist cell that caused all this capital misery. This is a big-time cell operation. A network of commerce cells that pretend to be legit, and won't quit. The winds of their corruption blew by everyone in the past years. No one heard a sound. Most were asleep while awake. These people are the really dangerous terrorists. The American politicians take an oath to protect the Constitution of a nation, but the terrorists don't take an oath to any nation. It's getting harder and harder to distinguish between who are the bad guys and who are the really bad dudes?

The Disappearance of Oversight

It's funny "ha ha" in a way, what some of the things this nation chooses to regulate that is of top priority. For example, the financial industry of plenty has so many laws and penalties for you and me that are totally incomprehensible. Regulations galore! If we, the citizens, step out of line with a simple case of bouncing a check, in some cases, you could be arrested! Don't even mention not paying your taxes on time. Penalties stack up on you like ants on a cake.

Yet, the rules that the politicians' lawyers create for the big-shot bankers frees them of accountability, and are a nuisance to the customer as it is planned to be.

If the oversight committees had not fallen in love with their degrees, and actually came to the realization that they could get off of their fat fannies and work for their pay to make a difference, that would have been a nice change of pace. (Oh, I forgot. Why work when you can get paid for not working?) They just so happened to be on a long vacation when all this disruption took place. Yeah, right! These Jaspers of the credit rating agencies worked for the companies that they were rating. I read that only a few people rate the entire stock market products for certain companies and states. That sounds like racketeering to me. Is that too harsh of a word to use when describing this configuration? Certainly it's a major conflict of interest. Now that's better, right? The sweet rewards of having the right diploma.

All kidding aside, there were no adults to be found in this whole financial massacre. Everybody and everything, living or not, was sacrificed. There is no escaping the wrath of these clowns. Now, all the power players claim that this was not their fault. Well, my question to them is, did you perhaps have a little bit to do with the nation going into decay, since you and others were in charge were responsible for guiding this economic ship to safe harbor? The press room is silent. A ten-year-old could have done a better job. Now, at this late date, the rating agencies want the glory of being seen as a responsible operation. "These are the men and women that you can bet your last dollar on," they say. You would lose that bet.

By the way, where was that fine trustworthy organization, the IRS, during all these explosions? They never said a word. Maybe it's because they acquired a home loan division during the boom, and sold it before everything went bust. That may keep them from investigating the subprime slime scam, especially if they had skin in the phony paper game. There must be some reason this whole event evaded the hawks at the IRS. It's probably just the same excuse that every other watchdog group is using for being MIA on this big breakup. Who knew?

If the IRS is organized enough to catch you for being late on your taxes, how could they have missed the largest economic cliff dive in history? They usually are not late on a date when it comes to checking on your finances. Then, there's the perception of a solid banking system, but we all know that's not true. Nod, nod, wink, wink. Then, there's the largest book of regulations in the country, keeping the yardstick on your behind to make sure you never get out of line. Only the dictators can set the measurement of law on you, and not the other way around. Let's be clear about that last point. You could use a bailout right about now your damn self, right? Remember the money the big banks stole from the people? "This ain't no bailout." I've said many times, it was a "go to hell route" for the good folks of America and the world, you know, the ol' "loot and scoot."

You, the citizens of this once-great empire, have been squeezed out of the equation by fat cat bank "greed-ors." The balance can be restored by realizing that the people who gave us this emergency cannot get us out of this unregulated den of digression. The only way back from this living hell is through truth. This was no act of God. This was an act of fraud.

Rush to Failure

Speaking of which, I must say something about the king empire killers themselves, the George W. Bush administration. First, let me state that I am a political atheist. With good reason to be so. One reason for example, is that democracy is so politicized that there's no solid ground of truth to stand anywhere. As the old joke goes, "If America had more than one major political party, I would vote." The next reason is stated by one of my favorite philosophers. Alfred Montapert wrote in his 1970 book, *The Supreme Philosophy of Man: The Laws of Life,* "The greatest threat to a nation is not the foreign government, but a growing dependence of the people on a paternalistic government. A nation is no stronger than its people." Unquote.

It just so happens that G.W. was at the helm during the most crucial moment in U.S. economic history. Civilization's very future hung in the balance as the new millennium opened in 2000. These economic "freak-o-nomic" drag kings pretending they knew about the financial facts when they didn't, is nefarious to say the least, and unprofessional and rotten to say the most. Maybe the nation should have hired the accounting firm of Price Waterhouse. They seem to do a good job of keeping track of the number of votes at the celebrity award shows. Why not? Nothing else seems to be working. I always ask people to name one great feat that globalization did for America, and not one person has to even think long. The answer for many years has been the same. "Not a damn thing!" Don't just take my word for it; look at the U.S. Census Bureau report for the year 2008. It's a chilling rundown of the total and utter disaster that the administration, Congress, and Wall Street gave us. Nice folks! Look at the numbers.

In this case the jury is in, and the report stated that this country has been in economic decline for the last eight years. The empire has been stripped of its wealth and worth. We have more poor people in the U.S. than ever before in history. So you see, there is a connection to this administration and the turmoil the world is living through. We are still living in Dick Cheney and George W. Bush's third term as presidential supervisors and emperors of the Executive Office. We are going through another lost decade. Doesn't it feel like it?

America got stuck in the mud trying to live in old colonial times. Now don't get me wrong, some of these ingrates in the financial world were turning more tricks with the stock market than a fox on a dollar block in L.A. It's a multi-layered contraption. It's not just at the top of the structure of finance where the hands of distrust coexist. It's also the middle to the lower levels that mix the pot of green goo as well. Sometimes I get the distinct impression that neither the Wall Street nor the 'Bush-o-nomics' crew had a clue what hit the economy. They all were walking around in fantasyland, thinking that everything was under control. In some ways, the very things that the multinational corporations and the Cheney administration desired, such as Iraq and Afghanistan, was the very focus that threw America off track. I guess at that time no one was minding the golden eggs. Actually, I think the surplus that Bill Clinton left for the nation was comprised from early on in the inaccurate accounting schemes from the White House and Wall Street firms. Let the bailouts begin! They bailed themselves out from day one. Just a theory.

Understand that Bush just happened to be the leader of the free world at the time the big economic bombs explode. This guy and crew love to be associated with bombs going off. Remember Shock and Awe? I don't care what their names are; I'm more concerned with their responsibility to their oaths. I've never read about an honest president anyway, so who cares about their reputation? They don't, because if they did, they would have honored the contract that they pledged to uphold. The treason these people sleep with at night never ceases to amaze me.

There were many scandalous reports that leaked out during the Georgy Porgy Era about the "I bear no responsibility crowd." One in particular that comes to mind was in 2008, when all of the governors of America sued the federal government for blowing the flames of the subprime housing fandango, by supporting the big banks to issue these bogus loans and spread this garbage over the entire planet. The Bush administration countersued, and won based on an obscure law from long ago. So the onslaught went on to new heights, and the public went to the dogs. The real estate industry is the only game in town that can support a military monster machine the size of America's. Technology can't do it, commodities ... nope. So, when you want to have wars on two fronts, you need a lot of dough. Welcome, you have just entered the world of,

"Let's clean out the peoples' bank accounts for idiotic pranks and follies." There was a lack of critical thinking that caused these war invasions of vengeance, and these taxpayers' spending sprees.

I'm not saying Bush and his fine-feathered crew are the only ones to blame, because there's plenty to go around. From the Demo-rats, to the lobbyists, to other gutless wonders. There are some innocent politicians and Wall Street folks, but they had been shut down completely. Call me a liar about my current observations, and I'll just calmly say to you, "Look around and tell me what you see." Better yet, I'm scared of you if you can't see the upheaval that's happened. What was gained by all the backdoor illegal, crooked, dirty dealing on Wall Street and the Washington White House Casino? Little gains for some and squat for others. That was a brilliant strategy like every other idea these people cooked up. Not!

From the devastating war invasions of choice that are still coasting along and milking the taxpayers for billions for eons to come. How could they possibly believe that the administration had no hand in this eclipse of financial destruction? The bought-and-paid-for media is proud to announce that this is a so-called fact, but I disagree. So much for that Red State/Blue State crap. A lot of good that propaganda did. You are laid off, the mortgage on your home is probably upside down, or you're homeless, whether you are from a blue state or a red state. That was total nonsense. It's time for the ones who know the lowdown of the crash game to step forward now. Most people were left out of the game when it came to watching the Wall Street Seduction plot. It was juicy and still is.

Learn and Burn

I couldn't imagine even starting to try to figure out what the fiscal system has thrown up at our bank account's doorsteps. The funny thing is (at least it would be funny if it weren't so sad), is that the monetary missionaries who created this fiasco didn't have their minds on the former profit-making machine: Wall Street. They were all over the map. No focus on the primary issues. The heartbeat of the markets is growing faint now. Not many money medics notice the conditions of failure spreading rapidly throughout the markets.

Let's not kid ourselves; this resourceful market has been dominated by single-vision lobbyists for decades now. They were only concerned with their political pastimes which created the perfect storm of the financial disorder. The largest public needs were never at the top of their list. I knew we were lost, but this is outrageous. I went cuckoo when I heard Henry Paulson, Treasury Secretary under George W. Bush, say after the crunch that the economy was stable. I knew differently, and so did a few others.

During the last years of the Bush administration, the medals of achievement to his posse were being generously donated to his cronies, while the company line on the economic outlook was that "We are in a rough patch right now, but we will get through this." I even think Paulson himself might have received an accolade from the old 'Bushmeister' for an economic ship well guided. I know

Alan "Greedspan" Greenspan received a medal of achievement from his buddies.

Now, Paulson, there is a man you can trust. Just listen to Hank's words, and you too can become mesmerized by the entangled hog slop spewing out of his mouth. He fits like a glove, perfectly for how this bunch of non-visionaries guided the craft astray, causing irreparable damage. If only this Bush/Cheney cabal had run for office in Iraq. Iraq is their land of promise, not mine. As a matter of fact, I'm tired of hearing about Iraq and the Middle East. I do wish people in general well, but sometimes you have to take care of number one! The "Bushites" could have run against Saddam in an election over there, and may the best rat win.

The multinational corporations bought the Middle East anyway, and we are still paying heavily for the purchase price. Can Americans own land in Iraq or Afghanistan? We should be able to, as much as we have invested our blood, sweat, and tears. Who am I kidding? We can't even put up an American flag in the downtown square of any one of these places, even after all of our spilled blood and lost treasures. Now, that is a dismal fact. That's really bad symbology for the American political parties. They scream we must have liberty, justice, and democracy for all, which translates into spend, spend, spend! Wall Street responded like the parrots that they are by repeating their holy mantra, "If the president said it, it must be so." At least we know that the consequences of the Street's actions brought about these economic results.

The Glory or the Money

The Wall Street subprime slime syndicate set up this attitude throughout the ranks that there would be no consequences for any action, good or disastrous. These stock market servants had a purpose of extremism, with no mention of any accountability. What these robbers have allowed to happen on their watch, while no one is paying the cost for, is this. Imagine traveling from the east coast to the west coast and never having to stop for a red light or a stop sign for the entire trip. What are the chances of that happening? Zero! Let these guys at the Street or the White House tell the story, and you'll hear about how their friends make that kind of a trip like that at least once or twice a week. That's my point.

For all of you sports fans, let's also say these are the same folks that would be on the first team in history to ever play a complete basketball game without committing a foul. Not one! Now, what they have done to the financial system is the same as a basketball team playing an entire season, including the playoffs, without the team ever committed one single foul. Never did a thing wrong. Now, that I think of it, let's just call it what it is. They played their whole career, and never got a foul called on the team. The only way that could happen is there was no oversight anywhere to be found on the White House and Wall Street premises from the regulators.

Between the Bush bravado about the ownership society and the whole hog or nothing approach, they represented only themselves and the big banks. They have also left a distrustful taste in the people's mouths. The instability the masses instinctively feel is a factual event, an economic wave of fluctuating inconclusiveness. With so many political hands in the cookie jar, there was not even a crumb left for Main Street to eat. As I said earlier, "The greatest crooks graduated from the greatest colleges!"

III
WALL STREET MEETS THE GHETTO

THERE ARE THOSE WHO FOLLOW the market for its intrinsic investment value, and others who only screen the market for its creditworthiness and validity. The latter fits me just fine. So, the summer of '07 was a nervous time for me. There was so much misinformation spilling out of the commentators' mouths about the misleading facts and figures of the slamdown. Not much about the oncoming credit wreck was being mentioned at this time until after the fact. They never sounded disturbed. It's hard to get the TV commentators to show emotion about anything that matters. This was no normal eruption in the summer of 2007 when the credit crunch was detonated. Some idiots were walking around shouting "viva la credit crunch!" like it was a fun non-eventful day (most likely a member of the Slick Dick Cheney fan club ... the master of the deficits don't matter crowd). I knew better.

You know, from a distance these bankers and politicians could pass for leaders, but under closer observation you see them for what they are. Lost souls. I remember having an eerie feeling in my gut about the blowback of the crunch. Wall Street was business as usual. On the TV shows at that time, most of the on-air personalities didn't know how to interpret this critical emergency. Sometimes, there were jokes and giggling. Remember, this was at a time when the wealth illusion was still in full effect in 2007.

A lot of people still thought that their wealth had increased. Just the opposite had happened. Their debt had expanded.

The prevailing winds of thoughts during this time were that "This too shall pass. We were going to have some rough patches," as the Commander in Chief Bush used to say, "but we'll be OK." So a lot of economists, analysts, and TV commentators just kind of took things in stride and accepted the company line. Many days, I screamed at the top of my lungs at the TV or the computer about the credit crunch being an ominous event. My wife was sure I had economic Tourette's while I was cursing and swearing. There was almost never any panic anywhere to be found on the radio and TV airwaves. I knew these guys and girls who were bringing you the financial news were slow-to-go in most cases, and this was no time for nonsense. The corporations would chant together, "It takes money to make money." What they really meant was, "It takes your money to make them money."

By this time, Wall Street was hitting the wall, and was headed straight for the ghetto, crossing the tracks to nowhere. The stock exchange and the White House had the classic symptoms of a patient with a ghetto mentality. Back in the days in my neighborhood, it was a running joke that if a pimp had a fancy gangster Cadillac but no money to put gas in the tank, that was a ghetto game. If you were dressed to the nines, had a pimped-out ride to match, but had no place to live and no cash to put fuel in the tank, then that is a ghetto mentality. Looks can be deceiving.

The past and current administrations, along with Wall

Street, all three have a ghetto mentality. America and the economy are barely just surviving this financial teardown, and both parties are just continuing with the big-spending mentality. This will change. In all fairness, there were some TV guests who were well qualified, and some respected economic professionals who were out in front on this story. They gave the audience a straight deal. There were not many. Most on-air folks in 2007 were swallowed up in self-congratulation and fantasyland truths, while a ginormous capital octopus was going down in flames, with tentacles left burning on every point on the planet's seabed. They saw it, but they just couldn't bring themselves to slam the Bush administration involving this breakdown or Wall Street.

This was a tough call, because what the media says really does influence the market. So many times they had to be careful of what they were saying. A lot of cute mind games were being played to fool the public. All the time I asked myself, where are the legit business people? The Wall Street model is breaking down into a fancy slum. Now, it simply has evolved into some kind of economic origami, taking a form of one thing and making it into as many shapes as possible is the Wall Street derivative's motto at this stage in the drama. Sounds exactly like credit default swaps mission, right? Now, no one really understands the financial platforms presently offered. They have transformed Wall Street into the Ghetto for Greenbacks.

The Threat to Civilization

Did you hear the infamous tale of truth back in September 2008, during the Dick Cheney days? Then-U.S. Treasury

Chairman, Hank Paulson, threatened Congress with a claim of imminent collapse and martial law coming to America's shores. I probably died a few lifetimes just living through these chilling times; were you there in your awareness? After an announcement such as this, how I could not lose it? I fell out of my chair reading this. (This is it! Imminent danger!) He said worldwide financial collapse was imminent if the bailout legislation was not passed. These big corporate giants are too big to fail. My opinion is that they were too big to succeed. This reported story is one for the ages. This was the moment when Wall Street met the ghetto, in this author's opinion.

Politicians like to scare the public with the word "imminent." But I can truly testify that in this financial case, the word was not overused or exaggerated. Paulson was telling the whole truth. We were going down! Many who paid attention knew this to be so. The bailouts were temporary, and delayed the inevitable. Now, everything is economically broken and falling apart. There's major financial structural damage to the system. The United States is turning into skid row for those with eyes to investigate. The most astonishing and appalling facts about the death of these American stalwart multinational companies is that many times, the decision to chart the very near future existence of these businesses' destiny was done over such a short period of time, that it could be classified as shocking!

Get this: The hotly contested arguments and agreements were not tackled over the timeframe of one week, not even three months or a year for these historic and iconic firms' economic survival. They did the cramdown over one weekend, Friday night through Sunday! The point I'm taking across here is this: That is how close we were in the fall of 2008 to a total collapse of the entire global investment network. I called them the beer, cigar and pizza pain party crew. If they came out alive, we live to tell about it another day, and if not, we're going to join them very soon, becoming the permanently underprivileged. This is known as kicking the can down the road until they could get out of office. Who wants to get the blame? Talk about economic origami. They were slicing and dicing our economy up like an economic sushi special. Buyer beware of the dish they served to the masses.

I believe the credit crunch was one of the most pivotal moments in the history of the entire world. The financial world shook as it never had before. The credit markets froze like a wooly mammoth in the last Ice Age. The remains from the freeze have yet to be discovered. The so-called smart ones were walking around in a daze, wondering why the big bang of bucks had been suspended, and punished the class of money makers and dollar shakers. This could not be what they spouted in their narrow visions. They wailed, "We are the class of influence! We are the masters of the universe!" This was not to be so.

By this time, the very foundation of everything that they had built their lives upon was crashing down right before their off shore bank accounts, for all to see. It was a humbling return point of humility for them: The big wigs at the banks and loan companies landing back down to earth. Boom! Did you hear that crash? That's their egos hitting bottom. Their egos needed as much deflating as the housing market itself did. They are too numerous to name, but their ship had sunk and now we all might be going down with them now.

For a reference point in time, I'm still dealing with the aftershocks of the credit crunch during the fall of 2007 and the collapse of 2008. We have not even been declared to be in a recession yet by the economists during this time layout. That was still at least five months away officially. December 2007 was the official start of the recession, but it would not be called a recession by economists until December 2008.

For my take on this matter, call it the recession or whatever you want, something nefarious started that summer of 2007. When the crunch blindsided the market, the masses' rapid fiscal pain begin to spread and leak out. This means that all of 2008 was spent in a recession/depression, and these money clowns on TV and in politics told everybody through all of 2008 that we would pull through this bump in the road just fine. You can find all of them, the politicians, financial TV hosts, and especially the Wall Street know-it-alls, saying, "Don't worry, be happy" on YouTube. (Goldilocks is dead!)

The Boom Went Za-Boom!

The structures started to collapse on Wall Street in 2008 just as it had in the Iraq and Afghanistan Wars. The financial terror could be felt from countries far away. I did not know what I was witnessing but it felt odd. The corporate symbols of the modern commercial world were starting to buckle like a bridge in a hyper-quake. The bottom of the wall on Wall Street was so shaky that at one point, no one thought the Street would last. It didn't, in its current form. My heart was beating at a rapid pace, an out-of-body experience. I couldn't sleep at night; I would pace in the daytime trying to comprehend what all just happen. Just then, another blow to the market by some other corporate megagiant was tagged too big to fail, but did. What, here comes multiple too-big-to-fail companies dragging and struggling to get a taxpayer bailout. I said, "This ain't no bailout, this is a go–to-hell route!" for the many citizens of the world. If none of these clowns wanted to drive this supreme vehicle of finance and democracy to safety, they never should have sit behind the wheel. This ain't no test drive for crash dummies. Unfortunately, that is what we got.

Crash Dummies and a Great Crash

As the momentum quickened, not many knew what the solution was to stopping this manufactured synthetic money implosion. Businesses were bleeding as they became the hunted. The workers on the Wall Street were showing much panic as this unsuspecting wall of unemployment came approaching at warp speed. The stock market floor was nervous with daily anticipation of which multinational enterprise would tank next. Internationally renowned companies such as Bear Stearns, Countrywide, AIG, MBIA, and Bank of America were choking on their own economic vomit. Oh, did I mention Lehman Brothers, the earth shaker that caused a major freeze in the credit markets?

I had to just bring this up again. Even if Lehman Brothers were broken up into five other companies, any one of those companies would be large enough to cause the entire global financial systems to collapse. That should give you a clue about the scale and the size of this multinational operation we are dealing with here. There are many of these zombie corps around today. Many other mega-corps were grimacing as their invincible profiles became only a silhouette of what they use to be.

The mortgage meltdown, also known as the subprime slime, was here to destroy and did it ever. Volatility was running wild and setting new records. Fannie Mae, Freddie Mac and the FHA, the largest home loan corporations, were running out of steam fast and becoming insolvent. The market exploded partly because of a new kind of exotic economic instrument that the loan companies jammed down people's throats called derivatives. Basically, these financial vehicles were also known as credit default swaps or SIVs. They were also known as CDOs, LBO, MBOs, NDEs, OBEs, take your pick. Who cares what you call them, they were a bunch of 'bushcrap' regardless. What the mortgage lender did was simply package hundreds of home loans, wrapped in thousands of treasury bonds, and then merge those with thousands of subprime loans and sold this garbage with triple AAA ratings worldwide. This is a very simple definition, of course.

This event was and is a global diminishing of wealth. A deflationary spectacle. The irony is that no one had an answer for what the real value of these toxic loans was worth. Not being able to evaluate them, the subprime slime default just wreaked havoc on the market and set the stage for a future visit from the loan sharks to hijack cash from every bank account in America and the world. The banks are keeping their cash to pay off their debts because investors won't buy these toxic debts. This is a major symptom of the credit crunch. The commonly accepted figure for the worth of these credit default swaps of junk paper that disintegrated the market was a galactic $600 trillion. One day in the future this has to be accounted for on the banks' books ... maybe. This was the figure that was in vogue during the days of 2006 thru most of 2008. How will they correct this catastrophe waiting to blow up in our future faces? They can't!

How Much is a Trillion Dollars?

Now, my father-in-law, Bart Moitié, is a sharp guy when it comes to mathematics. Once he told me about a simple way to think about how much money is a trillion dollars. He said a million dollars is roughly a stack of hundred dollar bills stacked five feet high. A billion dollars is a stack of hundred dollar bills stacked about a mile high. A trillion dollars is a stack of hundred dollar bills place side-by-side from San Francisco to Los Angeles and back, which is roughly 700 miles both ways. One trillion dollars has 12 zeroes. A trillion one-dollar bills stacked on top of each other would reach nearly 68 thousand miles into space. One-third of the way to the moon!

A professor of math, John Allen Paulos of Temple University, said that if you spent a million dollars a day starting two thousand years ago, you would have only spent about three quarters of a trillion dollars today. He also said that a million seconds is about eleven-and-a-half days. A billion seconds is about thirty-two years, and a trillion seconds is about thirty-two thousand years. Three trillion seconds is about ninety-five thousand years. Big numbers to wrap your mind around. One would have to circumscribe the globe forty million times to travel about one trillion miles. When you see the figures in the financial articles about some budget has lost 200 billion or 400 billion dollars, know that 200 billion is the same as 2 trillion dollars; 400 billion is the same as 4 trillion.

Think about this number. At this writing, the U.S. empire's debt is a little over 14 trillion dollars and growing. It's only 400 billion dollars under the Gross Domestic Product, a ratio of 97 percent. In the previous paragraph, I cited a figure that was being used in relation to the debt of the exotic loan market, alias derivatives. That is nearly 600 trillion dollars waiting to blow up in our faces. This money is hiding some-where deep in the underground basement vault of Wall Street, never to be seen again. "Help, we are choking down here!" the banksters scream for air before surrendering to the constricting death of credit default swaps, squeezing the life out of their bank books ... and our checking and saving accounts and retirement accounts.

What Could Possibly Go Wrong?

"Real estate always goes up in value" was the motto back in the day. Not so! Foreclosures of homes skyrocketed in 2006, which hurt the very heartbeat of every financial system. As the home values declined, Wall Street was having withdrawals greater than that of any highly stressed-out money addict. The real estate crunch was engaged in a full-scale freeze. All systems were begging to revert back to an earlier time of semi-order when people could have slight faith that their retirement would be there when they called it a day, kicked up their boots, and drifted off into the sunset. A time when the banks were not falling like abducted cows, dropped out of the sky from a UFO. Instead, disorder was the rule of the day. A time when a history of deleveraging waves crashed over the walls of Wall Street. A time when the blind led the blind. Murphy's law was in full effect: Whatever could go wrong did go wrong. The era of arrogance and ignorance was cemented in economic history. The perfect storm was brewing in everyone's non-waterproof bank accounts. This was no time to be in denial, but sadly many commentators and policy makers leading this sad ship off course were and still are in that state.

If there ever was a time for a clever plot to get us out of this nest of mayhem, now is the time to straighten up and fly right. Sadly, we have had no such luck. Self-delusion is still the top commodity of the moment. There are serial repeaters on the profiteering ship of money doom. The freeze of the stock market created colossal counter-party risk the likes of which the world has never been seen before. Counterparty risk simply means that the big banks, lending companies, and many corporations are all interconnected so closely that if one goes down then they all could potentially go bust. Every economic entity would become disabled also including your banks. The global financial enterprise would become officially defunct. This involved massive banks, lending companies, and insurance companies on the brink of no return. Bank of America, Wells Fargo, Citibank, MBIA, AIG, Ambac, all making thunderous bankrupting groans, screaming, "Rescue me ...

or else!"

Then enters the U. S. Treasury Department to the rescue with more taxpayer money offered to more big banks than you can count. A lot of private citizens could use a bailout their own damn selves right about now. We can only dream about our futures fund remaining with the public. The so-called Bush Stimulus Plan, later to become known as TARP (Troubled Assets Relief Program), still amounts to the S.O.S. The taxpayer is getting screwed! This was the crackup of the free market system. SIV was one of the first programs to offer the large corporate gangs assistance; translated: "Time to rob the common suckers' savings. We're running on broke. It's better for Joe Public to have no funds than the Wall Street bunch. We're just better human beings than they are. Never forget we are smarter than they are. That's why the masses elect us to create these chaotic times we live in." That makes about as much sense as a pig dancing in a fire pit. Why would the people want to elect a group of idiots? If they were lame idiots, why would they run for office or become head of these giant corporations? Power. As Lord Acton so correctly observed: "Power tends to corrupt, and absolute power corrupts absolutely."

Guess what? These losers are still making economic policy today. Maybe they've actually returned to their common sense by now. Well, no. They never had any to begin with. Here's their latest plan: Charge! To the rescue! Only the rescue is not for you or me, but for the Cool Hand Luke banker types. The cavalry is too late. They may shout, "Here's a credit card to pay off the government's debt of over $12 trillion budget, and still lifting off into space." China and Japan are the deciders of the nation's credit card's expiration date. Every stock market indicator that seems to show that any financial success of today is basically a "Dead Cat Bounce." This phrase comes from the example of a cat that has fallen off of a building that seems to bounce up right away and continue on only to die seconds or minutes later. Anything will bounce once. Just like the market!

Looking in the Rear View Mirror

In the meantime, the danger no one was allowed to speak about is the warning of systematic corruption. We are staring into the abyss of no less than a failed external control system. A new model is emerging as the standard of the near true future. I'll have more to say on that topic in a later chapter. I hope I have given you somewhat of a insight as to what was going on in the summer of 2007, when the credit crunch happened and the world changed forever, and in 2008, when all hell broke out. I came into the game chasing this sadness of madness when the Dow was a little over 14,000. I stopped investigating the stock market after 2008. There was no reason to further my inquiry. I came, I saw, I know … now.

The very same tragedy that overwhelmed the market in 2007, the credit crunch, was unspoken of in reporting in 2009, when I started writing this book. On the anniversary of the crunch in August 2009, there was hardly a peep from the press. More disappointing is the media's conceit and disregard for the significance of the crackup of the free market enterprise system. I watched the press, the Fed, the stock exchange and the White House all miss this game changing commotion. All of the politicians, with the exception of Ron Paul and a few others, were brain dead on this fiscal foolery.

The same is true for TV pundits that continue to front for the system currently. They didn't realize how deep the Bush knife of strife cuts was going to go. Those cuts went in so deep into their financial backs, they still don't know if their bank accounts are just bleeding or dying from all his lying. They were wrong before the crunch, and they were erroneous during the crunch, and they were definitely misguided after the crunch.

Oh, the crunch is still crunching! The credit crunch has damaged the mentality of the American people, and the fabric of the international bartering system of trade and commerce. They have effectively erased our financial strength, maybe forever. So when these historic corporate firms are collapsing all around you, there's nowhere to hide if you have been paying attention. Even if you haven't been keeping up with the latest, these contagious, immense house of cards are rumbling and tumbling. These firms are sizeable enough to take the fabled Atlantis down, so what chance does modern mundanians have of stepping aside to avoid this fate?

They have left humanity the ultimate task. No one can protect us from what lessons we must learn. There were loan speculators running a number on the good folks. They sold their products to an uninformed buyer and the clients bought it. Now, what's next? Just remember, this ain't Atlantis. This is America and we can change the outcome. I will expand on this subject in a later chapter of hope.

Casino Wallette

This was a multispectrum money-grabbing game. A Wall Street placebo effect in action. Now you have your funds and now you don't. On days when I was freaking out watching the budgetary roof on fire, the money puppets were saying, "We don't need no water, let the MF burn," to borrow a line from of one of my favorite '70s funk band, Parliament. It actually was like living in a burning inferno. It was like a Twilight Zone flick, where the ghost of Wall Street had appeared and charged the system with contempt of ethics. It was a discotheque on fire … or more like a casino. That's all it was. A casino without all the blinking lights. At least at the casino, the public can visit the premises and lose the money they choose to. Maybe, Wall Street should open up its stock exchange floors and put in some flickering lights, blackjack tables, and slot machines. Then if the folks wanted to gamble their life savings away, at least they would know what happened to their dollars, why their funds went up in smoke. Right now you have no idea about what happened to your funds.

The economic casino is much more dangerous than a standard casino. Most folks don't gamble away their life savings. They usually hold a little something back for a rainy day. Right? Well that's where the government comes in, which is Wall Street in drag. They lift all of your rainy day retirement funds and your extra pay-to-play money too. Like my momma used to say, "'Dem thieves get ya going and coming." Not so fast! Remember the casino, I mean the Alamo, I mean the Wall Street greenback light show.

The way the system works is basically, some low-level, unknown person is your liaison to your retirement or pension savings accounts, never claiming to be one of high esteem. This is who you're giving your hard earned dough to. I think not! Their line was, "If you give me your life savings and trust me, everything will be fine." They claim that they have all your financial concerns under control. They express through their false promises on company letterhead that the growth of your funds is their number one goal. You're in great hands. It's more frightening to think they and the world see this as a safe financial nonevent. The public must become more informed about these life-changing issues of today. I say this is the one of the most misunderstood milestones ever to face human comprehension. They don't teach you how Wall Street works when you're in elementary school—or even high school—for a reason. Why not? The kids could probably do a better job at managing the bookkeeping of the nation's funds once they understood how the system should work. We must have a better knowledge of how to keep our money for ourselves.

U.S.A. Stock Market of 2008

So, there I was, having a difficult time first of all trying to explain to myself; how do I recognize a stock market crash? Nobody was talking about the crash on the air-waves when it first began. At this time, the Golden Child Obama was about to accept the office of the president, so no one wanted to let the people know that the stock market had crashed. The market is so large and entangled that it can be incomprehensible.

So I kept asking myself in 2008, when not many were saying the stock market collapsed, what does a modern-day stock market crash look like, and how I do explain it in layman's terms? I meditated on a way to accomplish this task, and became inspired with a novel path to create a simple system of analyzing what a Wall Street crash would look like. Remember, during this time, the official position of the media and Washington was just "Relax. Nothing is wrong with the economy. Just hold on. Soon things will be fine." I knew different. Here's why.

The formula for numbers demonstrating the structural breakdown of a system I envisioned and activated was a revaluation of the Dow Jones Industrial Average's daily numbers. I started with the dates of January 1, 2008, through August 31, 2008, and I determine that the stock market was open for business 159 days of that year, up until that point. Next, I set up categories of number groups. The ground rules were the following: Out of the 159 days, I indicated how many days were up in the market, how many were down, or and how many were flat in the exchange. What I came up with was staring me in the face. Some sort of market decomposition was upon us.

When I say there was a flat day, my measurement guidelines were that the Dow was either 25 to 50 points higher or lower than the previous day's closing bell. During the days when the Dow appeared fictionally healthy, fifty points up or down was just a nonstarter conversation. When the Dow was at 14K and had some mechanics of fundamentals, everybody yawned when the market only moved 25 to 50 points in either direction.

Of those 159 days starting in January 2008, the market was down 70 days of that 159-day time period; 51 of the days were flat in the market, and just 38 were up. When I say the Dow was up in the market, there was no leadership in the movement of the exchange so the movement was just barely up. The pattern was becoming clearer. Instability abounded, hence, my call that the stock market crashed in the summer or fall of 2008. Now, I would feel a lot more comfortable if the combined 89 days that the market was either down or flat was just the reverse of the days the market was up, which were 38. In other words, a healthy stock exchange should be indicating that 89 of those days were up in the market and only 38 were down or flat.

There were days in the market during the fall of the year 2008 when the stock exchange would swing wildly 700 to 1,000 points in the red, and the bounce back into a correction that same day. My observation of these extreme point swings is that this is when the market lost its importance as a system of finance. In the spring 2010, that seemed highly unlikely to happen. These days if the market was to drop a thousand points, the financial markets would probably not recover. Many cycles into the future would be affected by this event.

Time will tell if my simple ideas and observations are correct. I suspect that one day we all will hear the grand announcement that the U.S. economist have come to an agreement that the stock market crashed in the year of 2008. If they really want to seem like they know what they are talking about, they will get more specific and say the fall of 2008 was when the decomposition of the commerce exchange occurred. I'm starting to sound like an economist. Somebody help me!

Card Fraud

Speaking of a casino, there's no gambling syndicate more ambitious than the grim industry of under-controlled credit card conglomerates. The leading reason people are in debt is connected directly to the magic cards of credit. I remember one of the things my former jazz instructor, the late, great clarinetist, Alvin Batiste said. He laid it down like this: "Credit is a black man's way back to slavery." We can broaden that comment somewhat, and say that credit is any man or woman's way back to slavery, regardless of color. Let's hope he's not right. He was a visionary and leader. We'll just have to wait and see. Not too long to wait now, anyway. These racketeers in the money fee game cause more people to lose sleep and lose their health and well-being… more than any other inducement in the free world, which ain't free at all.

The "pay now or pay later" layout is what these buzzards are infamous for. Pecking a hole in your wallet is the rationale behind them authorizing the design instruments of slavery to you any way they can. Now that their insane money plots of unsound motives has swallowed up the profits from these overenthusiastic crackpot "corpo-rapetors," the house that the Fed built has been burnt to the ground from the roof down. The Wall Street fire is precisely the reason for the taxpayer's financial decomposition, all presented to you by desperado credit card sharks. A shark is a shark!

So, let me get this straight. They lose most, if not all, of their money investing in con jobs and we the people must also get ripped off by having to repay any funds these rats may have been irresponsible with and can't account for right. Just checking. So the citizens are going to pay for the war invasions, the bailouts, the bankruptcies, and the credit card swindle. You can't forget about the car companies and dealerships going bust, and I didn't even mention the busting at the seams prisons. Oh, and the schools.

That's just to name a few, oh you can't forget about the individual states begging with palms up for the public to pay more taxes. Logic has left the building. In reality, we can never get out of financial debt, but we can get out of spiritual debt – I'll talk about that in a later chapter. So, there is no time, there is no money, there is no debt and there is no system. Well, unfortunately we are that sucker-rich public. The bank of last resort for the mega and regional banks. We will be stuck with their bills forever, even though we didn't get to enjoy the rewards.

Once in a Lifetime Deleveraging

Look folks, perhaps what we are witnessing here is a once-in-a-lifetime cycle. I might even be too hard on Cheney and the Bush tap dancers. Not! After reading "The Lost Decade" in the Wall Street Journal, there's no way I could be too hard on Cheney/Bush and the rest of their partners in crime. I'm possibly overly critical of the masters of Wall Street. Not, again! Now don't get me wrong, it's not that these misfits don't deserve getting slammed for their plethora of misdeeds. They fanned the flames of this fake Jake dollar dumper, but this may not be all not their fault. I know many say that you can't just blame one administration for the global economic blowup we're facing today because it goes back to previous administrations.

This is true. No United States administration is a shining example of fiscal and monetary ethics. Imagine what President Obama could have done with a budget surplus. Maybe even start more wars. Dummies can start wars. Some just did, but who can stop wars and start peace? That's where true genius lies, in my opinion. It seems like it would take some ingenious souls to activate peace again on this planet, and reestablish the necessary balance to control man's desire for material gains for the few. Every time this has been tried, it has failed - including this time around.

You didn't know that there is a federal bank of the people's branch located in your wallet or pocketbook, did you? Now you do! That's where the pickpockets hang out. Some might say that I am too critical of politicians. Not true. Some of these slap-on-the-back people are not living in the real world anyway. Right? You see, an honest politician will find it easy to work within the Constitutional framework laid out by the Founding Fathers. Renegades find this federal commitment totally intrusive to the operation of their multinational black government operations. Not being concerned with the nation's best interests at heart, just observe how these dark financial and bureaucratic zombies have burdened this once-great country, America, and the world with this possible economic downfall.

This is not a new story. The system went astray, or at

least the folks leading the front company of the U.S.A. went bonkers. A blastoff event happened back in 2007 through 2008, and to say that these were heated times is an understatement. Incomprehensible amounts of money were flying around the world at the speed of light, everywhere, at home and abroad. Remember the lands of the sands where trillions of dollars just disappeared into some desert oasis black hole? As many may already know, the former Secretary of Defense Donald Rumsfeld stated publicly the day before 9/11 that $2.3 trillion were wasted through widespread imperial dizziness (my words). Today, no one would stand by and watch this kind of loot being burned through without screaming at the top of their lungs.

These are hard economic days that we are presently experiencing. This act nowadays could be considered treasonous to lose that much diñero. Just think of what we could do with that weapon of mass corruption money loss now. We might even have money to keep the nation safer. What a difference a decade makes. There was monetary absurdity that surfaced during these times. Who knows where to recoup the squandering that went down back then? It would take divine intervention just to locate the records of this financial fandango, paying the cost to be the boss.

As the President of the United States, you have an obligation to leave the country in better shape than what you found it in. Is America safer today? Even an idiot can see that this is not the case! Good people are scrambling for their very existence everywhere. This is the question that not many head honchos even want to discuss today. After all of that propaganda about how they made the world safer, the facts have come home to roost.

It was a bunch of lip service. Just about any one of us regular citizens could have done the job at a higher level of efficiency, as long as we had a dose of integrity within us. That's what the Founders intended—a citizen government, not a government run by professional politicians. We could not have made it any worse than it is now. You would have to work hard to destroy a country of this size. No, you don't. You have to go on vacation a lot, and let things fall through the floor. Then the rot will eat through that floor and the entire infrastructure. Then you can certainly create the end result such as what we have today. As for Wall Street ethics, well, they were generally caught riding the politician's merry-go-round to nowhere's village. It's all too confusing now. I just felt a curious wave from all of the conspirators out there. Their eyes are bulging out of their sockets, asking, why is it so confusing? Only the uninformed don't know why they floated the vote to get themselves in office. The people in the know have the 411 why they lined up for federal employment, right? We the people were a means to an end.

One day, I was trying to understand what the reason was for this blinding deleveraging event that is occurring. Why so fast? Then a couple of thoughts came to mind: Primarily, this cycle of resetting the balance of financial power is not only an economic event, but a call for humanity to experience a conscious elevation conversion. We must get ahead of these deteriorating commercial consequences. This is the only way. Know all you can about the financial winds of today. "This is the big one!" as Fred Sanford from the TV sitcom Sanford and Son would say.

We could be looking at a financial fantasy gone awry of unimaginable fund depletion, the kind that the world has never seen before! Maybe a 300-year hypercapital counter investment crash cycle from centuries of overleveraging by the banks and leadership, or should I say, "Bleed-us-ship." We're just the lucky twerps who get to live through this cycle when it will have it greatest effects. A fiscal reality shapeshifting is happening. We are in a fast-motion brain blur. What we are dealing with here is not only the lost decades from the war tribes of the Bush administration, but also the lost centuries of Wall Street corporations deleveraging crimes starting to crash down on the folks. Just a theory.

The media needs to take the words "financial recovery" out of their vocabulary. There ain't been no economic recovery since I've been covering this crap. There ain't gonna be an economic recovery anytime soon, so forget about it! I'm overwhelmed and over leveraged myself. Now my personal infrastructure is starting to deleverage. It ain't a pretty sight. How could it be? I live in America, the playground of nonproductive pain.

What's Left to Fail

There really aren't many more significant industries left to fail. Deafening, vast, picture-perfect model companies have misrepresented themselves as worthy capitalistic investment safe havens. They were sadly only impersonating a success story. The big banks, the car makers, auto parts suppliers, the car dealerships, the insurance companies, the loan companies, those who blew up Wall Street, the policy makers, the military, real estate, and many more are soaked in the green blood of greed. Somebody got the loot! What's next to fall or who's next to fall? In some ways, I don't even care. I'm sick of the whole symbolism of idolatry of household company names that should be respected.

The spine-chilling monetary crumbling that occurred in 2007 when these giants started to uproot has just begun. Soon everyone will be gasping for some form of a normal life in the near future. This is a measurement of the true size of this gargantuan bubble that blew up in our faces. Unnecessarily, in this author's opinion. I'll have more to say on this in a later chapter called, "How We Could Have Avoided This?" We had no idea of the astronomical dollar figures that were being spent and wasted on our behalf … for their benefit. Now we're feeling the real consequences and ramifications of the "Raiders of the Found Arks'" actions. Plundering the peoples' treasures. This was cash embezzlement in the clear sight of the world's all-seeing eyes. The market crash can only be equal to the investment and the amount of pillaging, thievery that materializes from the cauldrons of many depraved, wicked little minds. Are you concerned yet?

Also, there's considerable mass agony to come. The Wall Street skeleton doesn't have a backbone anymore. When the Dow Jones is heading in one northern trajectory, the NASDAQ is moving in a southward orientation, and the other market markers are charting a eastward path, then I know it's time to ready myself for a different formula of life than what I'm have been accustomed to. I know for sure that the Dow Jones and the NASDAQ are supposed to move in sync with each other, in the same direction. I've seen it when I began scrutinizing the market with the Dow at 14,000. The economic jet stream today is shifting in peculiar ways. I leave you with this observation, my friends. Wall Street is but a shell of the former egotistical green monetary beast that it used to be, churning out profits and losses. Can Wall Street survive? Let's hope so but it ain't looking good right now. So, what's left to fail is something that only time will tell.

IV

THE GREATEST STORY NEVER SPOKEN

WHILE STOMPING THROUGH THE WOODS of the economic jungle of "Weird Street," lost and confused, I knew that I had a dedicated mission of intrigue and mystery. I was setting out to explore perhaps not just one of the greatest stories in humanity's history never spoken in my tongue and style, but in some ways maybe the last of the great stories worth telling. My early cosmic contemplations and earthly thoughts were begging for an answer to a certain question. How do I even begin to look for something so abstract as the blowup of a stock exchange during 2007? The media was camouflaging the facts. This was the standard rule of the day.

The financial fundamentals back in those days were slim to none on the banks' books. My posse on the internet said that because there are no fundamentals in the markets, a global financial pitfall is approaching fast. Your money will be vanishing, presto! ... right before your eyes. As a matter of fact, the juicy days of this whole economic breakdown were during late 2006 through 2008. Soon after this period the stress tests for the banks went into effect. Many instrumental investment banks lost considerable amounts of funds that they could not afford to lose during those mind-blowing times. There was no way to protect them from their misfortunes, which soon became our downgraded lifestyles. If we just could find those pesky market fundamentals buried deep under a crate somewhere in a dark Wall Street basement. Who knows? We might just find a way out this constrictive overshadowing departure from economic sanity.

During the year 2007, the stories on the net were inflamed and reaching a boiling stage. Criticism of the administration and the financial world at large were reaching a high point. This was even before the credit crunch had brought about its wrath of destruction. The national leadership had failed to conduct its affairs in a fiscally responsible and practical manner that works for the benefit of the citizenry. The system was putting up a front for the press that all was OK, so that the media would get off of their case.

What slowed the mass (mainstream) press down is the fact that this financial funk story kept leading back to the same targets: in the direction of the former president rent-a-wreck himself, Bush and staff, as well as many of the Wall Street elites. No one wanted to agitate the powers that be. So over time, as the blinds were lifted and retail investors started to see the light, they bailed out of the market with the fury of thunder and lightning in 2008, leaving the simmering disorder of finance in question of its termination. Who could blame them?

The acts of the financial leaders and the politicians must be consistent with the intent of their oath and the position being held by the peoples' servants. The year 2008 was when the empire's debt template was rewritten in stone. Primitive numbers from our archaic past were now beginning to determine our future opportunities for wealth. Never forget the Great Depression: a revisitation of a time when the stock market disappointed all who intruded into the land of make-believe. In other words, it was an ugly year for profits. By the time 2009 rolled around, the damage had been done. We are all just feeling and seeing the after-effects of "the age of the unconscious ego cycle" that dominated those months and years of 2000-08 and beyond.

This was a time to be remembered. It's like knowing where you were the day President John F. Kennedy was murdered, or Martin Luther King, Jr. was assassinated, or when Mahatma Gandhi was killed. All the important events of our time. This credit crunch is an unrecognized moment in American history and the world that will be more significant to the historical record books in the coming times of future financial cycles. Anyway, I'm trying to inform you that it's a sure bet that the results of this economic mismanagement will be on the way soon to a town near you.

I often ask myself, "Why me?" when it comes to writing this book. When I sit down and actually think about the answers to that question, I must include my oldest brother, Percy Rudell Johnson, in that conversation. He is still one of my heroes today. He was the first black fire captain of the Shreveport Louisiana Fire Department. He also was a musical genius to me. He played several instruments fluently. My little brother Gerard also is a multi-instrumentalist. I come from a very musical family. Percy died in the line of duty at a very young age. He was aware of many of society's problems, and was trying to correct some of the racism he believed was rampant in the department while he was the captain. What a guy. Once again trying to do good for the many. Like me.

I've also received some intuitive answers for that question, why me? Such as, perhaps I was an Atlantean, or maybe in another life I was a point man on an island or mountain that warned the tribe trouble was coming. It could be as simple as I'm a fool for even trying this. We may never know the answer to this because as a result of this investigation, my life has changed forever. As it should be. Sometimes change is good and bad. One thing I do know is that the scene is crazy by now and soon everybody will be joining in, pronto.

Then, there's the other side of my personality that tells me that I'm not loco. To prove it to myself, all I would have to do back in the day is to stare at the internet and see the mass economic confusion there and on the TV shows. Instantly, I'm relieved to know that I'm not living in a fantasy world. It's not me that is insane, it's them! The whole "wham bam, thank you ma'am" altitude of the poli-economic system of the hallucinating herd of pipe dreamers. They had not one speck of prudence when it came to retaining and preserving the frugality of the free market exchange system. It's been a long beat down emotionally for me since the crunch of '07, but I ain't that beat up. I know which directions that the winds of these financial fundamental disturbances are breezing in from. North, south, east and west. Those are also the same directions that your funds will blow out of your bank accounts soon!

Confession of a Recession Man

Here I was, going off to tackle one of the most humongous episodes in the minds of present-day mankind. Little ole me. A kid from a city of no acclaim. A driving resolve persisted within me because I kept asking myself, who was going to tell the people? I never got an answer in the early days, so I continued to dig deep into the inner workings of the Wall Street slutfest. You wanna talk about a nasty rim of existence. During this loss of the people's wealth, I was determined not to be a member of that group: The people of the lost. Guess what? That didn't work. I'm still lost, but it's a different kind of lost. It's not the kind of lost from not having enough information; it's more the kind of lost from having too much information. Boy, this ain't the kind of story you wanna rush home to tell your grandkids. This is the most difficult mission I've ever embarked upon.

Once again, my whole time researching this life changing event, America's fall from grace, something in my head kept asking, who's going to let the people know? Not the people who manufactured this dumb debacle. They are not the team you want in charge of your child's school PTA fundraiser if you want to have any funds left. The kitty will come up short with these characters. Just like our bank accounts are being trimmed today. The political process has failed the people who entrusted their leaders and the people failed the process by not making these servants of the Constitution qualify their reasons for such actions and continue to question the powers that be. We are nothing more than human shells if we don't rock the boat.

Right now as I write this book, there were not any manuals written on the financial crisis at the time that I started to investigate this subject. I just followed a different story at a different time than most people. There was no guide for me to collect the information I needed all in one place. I had to learn on the run. While on my journey I discovered that "the boat done sprung a leak, Captain! We're standing on shaky ground!" Use any metaphor you want to, but the point is, who is going the give the people the lowdown on where to look for the Wall Street Easter eggs that might explode in your pocketbook? The commander in chief. He's protecting the hustlers that are robbing us clean.

The law? Like I said, when the law only protects a few, there is no law. So we are on our own, especially because these control geeks are trying to bury the financial bodies so the scam continues. This is not a political event any more—this is a humanitarian involvement project. Even the authorities are labeling this as the worst economic crisis since the Great Depression. I say the credit crunch of '07 was the start of the Greater Depression. Everything else is just the results of that historic monetary freeze up.

Who's right and who's wrong was the main theme running through my burned-out mind daily. Listening to the TV wannabe genius talking heads in 2007 and 2008, I heard leaders being criticized for this paralysis of monetary policy. I watched tons of laws broken or being modified, while many market analysts agreed with the on-air personalities, that this too shall pass. The media was just as impacted as the rest of us. You would think they could discover where this trouble originated. They were guess-timating like everybody else.

The media was scared to look at the devil in the details of the corruption, so obvious for those with eyes to see. It was like the media was in some type of twilight zone stupor. The fog never lifted. Anyone who watches the local news only is missing the greatest story never whispered. The regional news commentators couldn't interpret the maze of a mess that had been created on the Street. We could be the most uninformed modern society that has ever existed. We've been thrown into the junkyard by multi-national corps. Now, it's a question of retaining what wealth we have materially and, most importantly, spiritually.

The financial empirical nightmare was still claiming success at this time, from December 2007 into '08. "Who knew?" is the backup line the leader bleeders like to use as an escape route for what went wrong when questioned about the facts. We are good people, and these bastards don't deserve such a one-way street of loyalty. Tell me what loyalty do we receive back from the system of economic policies? Zero! We are the heroes, and they are the zeroes. This ain't our fault. We all got shot in the back by pirate Banditos pillaging the U.S. treasuries. No adults were in the Wall Street or Washington rooms. The stock market TV pundits were talking more about how the new government fiscal stimulus plans worked. They are not even concentrating on companies' earnings and dividend fundamentals. Ah, remember the days when you could just talk about fundamentals in the market such as earnings and dividends? When stocks had credibility? Where did it all go astray? That is always a bad sign when conversations about stock market chaos rules over financial fundamental talk. The Main Street public is being bought for pennies on the dollar daily and they don't even know it. They are being foreclosed on, and deservedly so for some. Others didn't dream they could and would lose everything. Going from riches to rags is a whole new game of life.

People who have experienced natural disasters in most cases claim that the loss of their material gains doesn't matter to them, as long as they have their lives and their loved ones are safe. I agree and feel for them with all of my heart. I have one question, though. Why do they spend most of their lives collecting these things, only to dismiss their value when they are destroyed because of natural misfortunes? Wouldn't life be better if they had not put so much importance on things? Of course it would.

Modify and simplify your life now! Hanging out in nature is the true treasure anyway. Shallow temporary financial triumphs are falsehoods that restrict the destiny of the citizens. Looks like simple pleasures will become the rebel call of the day soon. Now don't get me wrong, I'm not saying that we don't need material comforts, but the excesses of the last decade were unsustainable. This was a man-made disaster.

It's better to fail at something through dedication and hard work, than it is to succeed at an operation that will eventually be defeated. It's going to take a colossal commitment to create a successful ending to this epic saga. I'm also writing about the "Too Big to Fail" motto that swallowed the banks and the United States' free market capital system whole. A prime example of succeeding at failing. Can you think of another rushed government announcement that claimed that the mission was accomplished, now only to see that broadcast deteriorate into the abyss along with the mission?

There are so many angles to this financial fallout. It's hard to know where to begin. I've been after this story for quite some time now. I only have time to read forward-looking articles. I never review past articles. I don't need to. I was there. Remember the times when people would talk about the Sixties? They would ask, were you there? The running joke was that if you remember the Sixties, you weren't there. Who could stand to be around all those dope-smoking, crazy hippies anyway?

For most people, the straight job was the America dream, or so they thought. If you look around at the corporate experiment today, many are not so sure that this was the way. They are horrified that their whole life may be a waste of time. The intelligentsia got it wrong! The same corporate world that hated the movement of the "be yourself crowd" has let you down. Be careful who you get educational advice from. Well, those loony hippies' way of life don't seem so ridiculous right now, compared to the unsustainable mess that the suits got us into. Just "tune in, turn on and drop out." After checking into this economic origami for years, that hippie motto fits me just swell right about now.

The Meek Will Not Inherit the Earth

At this time, the elected officials were living in a negative bubble world that was blinded by injustice. They were and, in some cases, still are today being treated as demigods and gladly accepted the comparison and any other accolades. Little do they know that their source of power is an illusionary authority. The meek will not inherit the earth, in their narrow view. They have very small-minded goals. They never looked around to observe and behold that the foundation of the American empire was being destroyed by the same elements that always erodes a nation's progress: corruption, deceitfulness, and fraudulent selfish manifestos. The delusional fools in charge, including the Federal Reserve, showed disdain for any discordant and different assessment than their recommendations.

The meek should inherit the Earth, in this author's opinion. These folks who exploded this economic bomb on the public had their shot, and look at what you got for mementoes. Another way of reflecting upon the meek gaining authority is to see it as an inner power. The ones who have worked hard to keep their hearts and souls clear of the ego's illusional power are destined for greatness. They did not go after the trying-to-be-rich kick. They stayed within their means, not the power-monger type who will step on anyone to get to the top like Tom Delay. I'm speaking about the meek who always had a helping hand for the other person. These are the powerful souls. If you are lucky enough to be one of these everyday angels, then may the glory and the magnificence of the Universe always support you.

Besides, aren't you tired of the same old power structures that were in charge until this financial carnage happened? These people have no new ideas for us to live by. Why not trust your own heart and mind? We tried the other way, and it did not work! So let's try some fresh perspectives. The gifts that are in store for the meek could be surprising for most who are decreed such an allotment. The reward for being an honest scholar is to inherit the Earth. The next life cycle of planetary transition will determine whether you are truly worthy to be considered among the meek. It maybe better at this time to be a common meek than to be a financial geek.

Man of Peace

I'm looking outside of my window today, and it's a beautiful sunny day. A part of me still does not want to claim that this phony paper game even exists. Guess what? It doesn't exist. That's the dilemma. It's the grand political and economic illusion. I never thought about a book writing project this on this or any other topic before, but I guess it had to be done. I had to put it down, pen to paper, so I could tell what little I knew about this enormous economic topic in type. It sure enough eased my mind to write this book of doubt and hope, but it's that old adage: Be careful what you wish for, you might just get it.

Look, I am a man of peace and creativity, not destruction. Life for me is about the preservation of all living creatures, large and small. I'm no dream breaker—I'm a dream maker. I always want people to see me the same as you would a weatherperson, reporting and tracking the financial storms. You wouldn't get angry at a meteorologist for reporting the current stormy weather. So, I tell people I'm just reporting the economic stormy weather. Same job, different topic. Folks can really get angry with me for informing them about the current financial conditions. I don't know why. I didn't cause their despair. You see, the weather people can forecast that a storm is coming and everyone tries to prepare the best they can for the event. The public sees this as a naturally occurring development. But tell them that a political party has caused the disappearance of the money, and they blame the reporter. Crazy how the civic-minded herds fit the facts to suit their own social leanings. I've taken plenty of heat for discussing this topic. I must be right!

I am a bass player who performs music and comedy for families in northern California along with my wife, Lori. I am by nature an easygoing fellow who doesn't like to deal with a lot of drama in my life. Boy, did I pick the wrong bone to gnaw on. This is the Wall Street drama-bama of all dramas. I can guarantee you that there are no other episodes of paramount concern in my life besides this lil' ole possible financial global collapse thing that's bugging me. Other than that, I'm fine. Really. I always try to be conscious of the other person's space, and not intrude in their alone-zone time. I'm not the soapbox kind of guy, where I just set up a station downtown and start blasting away with my diatribe about the world's woes. If you ask me, I'll tell you. The only true reason I'm writing this book is because I'm economically constipated and it needs to come out. To tell you a small lie, I feel better already. In some ways I feel better for maybe helping some people, and not as good because the boogie man won't leave the building where the money is being printed.

C'mon, I used to ask how long this monetary trash will keep going on? Now, many years and labor pains later, there's no need to ask that question anymore. It will never not go on. This blow away of the commercial system for me is like parenting a really bad child. They get bigger but not better. I really don't like playing this game of outsmart-the-crooks anymore. It's been years of playing detective, running the tips down from unsuspecting sources. Waiting for the next big mountain of debt to crumble. I am really tired now. I had no staff to help me clear the path of financial jungle of the banks who were shift shaping into forms only their worst nightmares could have imagined.

If I had to do it all over again, would I take the eight to twelve hours a day that I put into this years ago, just to have a comfort zone of recognizing when to pull up stakes and initialize my Plan B? Maybe, but it was a lonely existence. It was so funky, a dog on a gut wagon would gag inside of the Wall Street stock exchange doing those days. That's why you had to be able to rock and roll in the funkiness of the green dough game. I'm talking about the low-down dirty, nasty gizzards of Wall Street and government street. It ain't pretty.

I do recall making public service announcements during our shows. I'll take a few minutes to inform the public about relevant issues of finance. In 2008, I tried to book myself to speak on this topic in public local libraries. I sent flyers out to inform the public about this event and got zero response. Guess I was ahead of my time.

My Hall Of Records

Recently, the folks who had a hand in this debacle have written books and are going on tour trying to rewrite the nation's history. Too late for that! These people did not stop the problem. They are part of the problem. Many others saw these people's actions that caused the devastation when it was going down. I said all that, to say this. I created my own hall of records. Being one of the ones to call the market crash in 2008, I also have proof that I also called the recession in 2007. I recorded an eight-pack of audio CDs with dates on the recording in the fall of 2008 to verify not only the dates of the recording, but also reporting on the substantive actions of the stock market each day. I sent these CDs to some people I know all over the country and internationally, so they would have some kind of record of what happened, in this author's opinion. I also coined the phrase "The Greater Depression" earlier than anyone previously that I have heard. I have a recorded date as proof of that as well. Unless someone can prove an earlier date than my use of the phrase, I'll be glad to recognize their date if it predates my original recording.

I also have a library of about a few hundred articles of what I felt at the time was the best and most interesting commentary on the economic issues of the day. These articles literally take you on a journey from the first times when the market began to rumble and was on the brink. The actual credit crunch is also on paper from its beginning to the blow-up in July-August 2007. These writings probably date back into 2005 and go up to late 2008. I also recorded over two hundred TV financial shows, not just for information but also for comedic purposes, as I watched these TV talking heads get the call wrong time after time. I knew that I was on the right trail.

So, for some reason the urge to gather the records of this event and spread them around was an intuitive occurrence for me because of the other research that I had collected. This is the amount of research it took for me to get a handle on these current fabrications of financial misstatements. This time is different than any other economic cycle in the nation's history, so I had to beat my own doors down. I didn't know which door to knock on for another clue to this drama, but I just kept knocking until the right door opened. This has been an unbelievable journey. Maybe one day we'll have an opportunity to meet each other. When and if we do, I'll tell you about my story firsthand and show you my hall of records one day. In the meantime and in between time, this book will have to suffice as the next best source of information. Best of luck to you and yours in getting through this fiscal farce.

A Run on the People

It was a run on the people and still is. It's getting worse all the time, a soft war that now has turned into a full-scale economic guerilla hard war. This battle is striking the public's wealth and bringing the strife of a lifetime. We were sitting here like turkeys waiting to be plucked. The politicians were clucking and the banks did the plucking of your funds. The superior world of commerce for the few and no profit for the rest of the human goats is the first exploitation principle of slavery.

Many families are on the streets because of these non-visionary tribes of incompetence. The so-called vogue body politic. They let all the subjects down—across the spectrum. I often wonder what the politicians, Wall Street, and Joe and Jane Public will be doing the day when they discover that the bottom has fallen out and the banks will not be opening any time soon. Every financial instrument has been declared insolvent! We won't have long to wait and see now.

I've always said that it is better to break a family's heart with honest information than to let them get destroyed. One of my original mottos is "prepare before you curse and swear." I will continue to inform as many as I can about this oncoming tumult and unrest, but I'm only one man. Right now, because of the humongous underhanded debt dealings, you know, the ride in the grand leaders' deficit parade, the nation-state and the entire world has lost their entire moral monetary compass. People are feeling wobbly in their psychic daily existence. "Man, if they just would have legislated some laws against these creatures of habitual patterns of stealing the nation-state's riches, we might not be in this whale of a mess." There were already laws galore on the books to stop this kind of finagling from going on—just no enforcement of those laws were being applied. What politician or financial guy wants to arrest themselves and be the fall guy for protecting the Constitution of the civilized democracy, America, by squealing on a buddy who did wrong? None of these brave ones. Not the gatekeepers of a supposedly literate society of high finance.

You know you're living in warped dimensions when the enforcers of U.S. law are being misled by high ranking officers who don't know the economic lowdown themselves. They gotta read this book. Some know, and some don't. Most men and women are working for the right side of the justice patrol. Most of them want their families to co-exist in a nation of laws. It's just a few sad apples that want to make their cartoon dreams become a reality by claiming imperial political overreach. Their fantasies, if not put in check, will therefore bring unwarranted hostilities and struggle to all sovereign citizen masses.

I can remember walking around in the fall of 2009 thinking, "Wow, we just barely made it out of 2008." I didn't want 2009 to happen only because I knew the financial pain it would bring the people as a result from the shakedown of 2008. Apprehension about our future was causing a lot of uneasiness. I also felt even more concerned about the transition from 2009 into 2010. Being in tune to the moment helped me to also perceive that very disturbing economic news would be in the foul sulfuric smelling winds of 2010. Not just the oil, corexit, and methane winds from the British Petroleum oil disaster in the Gulf of Mexico, either! A wholesale budgetary suffering was headed our way. Our very banking lifeline was being held in the balance.

These are high stakes fiscal poker games these creeps are double-dealing out to us. Only the big dog investigators who were hunting down the credit crunch from the beginning can know the smell of this hunt now. We are getting closer to the kill. Put up or shut up! The time for lip city is over from these characters of monetary manipulation. Get lost, would you? I meditate and pray that the real visionaries will become recognized for who they truly are. They are standing up and stepping forward presently. These folks are here on our planet right now to help us get out of this. Listen to them. I might be one of them. Maybe? I'm not sure.

The Greed Goal Post

The latest extend-and-pretend exhibition of financial hopscotch by the federal system of green magicians is this: The economic stock market rules have been flung out of the windows. Your dollars and your babies' saving accounts have both been thrown out of the banks' windows along with the bath water. I want to discuss this topic because it is near and dear to me. During late 2008 into 2009, I had been informing some people of where I thought the currents of the market were headed. That was not an easy thing for me to do. Hey, my street cred was at stake. I was trying to make the call on this mucho-money letdown. Anyway, my calls on the underwriters of greenbacks were going belly up at certain times. My calls were coming into the financial landing pads off course. I knew I had done my homework chapter and verse on the markets, so what gives? Then it hit me just recently like a ton of golden rotten eggs!

I asked myself why the missed speculative predictions on my part were happening. The answer crystallized right before my inner eyes. The feds and the banking system are smashing and changing every rule that the standardized free market capitalistic enterprise system uses as a foundation to measure success by. In short, they were kicking the proverbial can, not only down the road, but off the cliff! Can you say Wiley Obama Coyote? So my calls were correct, but they kept moving the goal post. This stuff can already drive you batty, but the magic tricks they pull off adds another dimension to the misdeeds and misleads. Remember, the market hates uncertainty! That was the mantra of the day back then, and stills stands today. Take a panoramic view of the current government's big business sponsorships. Now that's subsidizing uncertainty! Desperate times call for desperate measures.

V

NEW WORLD FARTERS ... I MEAN, ORDER

"NEW WORLD ORDER!" This is a subject that is of interest to me only because of the fear that this phrase induces when folks and media outlets holler, "New World Order!" Are you scared yet? Can you scream that phraseology in a crowded theater and not get arrested? I don't know. Those are very auspicious and suspicious watchwords. Conspiratorial or not, the very utterance of this verbiage can make some folks nervous and spooked out in certain circles. Different societies have unusual names for this mirage of a power order. Many people may think that just because someone has been given a created title of globalist, it means that these likely miscreants are all superior-minded characters, but nothing could be farther from the truth.

These educated types are quite capable of mismanaging an entire global economic system. Look at this current mess influenced by these cheater leaders. We now are trying to squeeze blood money out of the economic rock piles they left in our bank accounts. They have made us invalid debtors to world finance for eons to come. They swapped our hard-earned cash for bailout slogans. We don't have many options to be optimistic about presently. We have fewer choices if we want to try and earn a living than ever before. Did their plan work? They don't know. Ask someone else.

Nowadays, anyone with a computer can probe into the shadows of what is called the New World Order. One question I have for the order is this: Should we address it as "A New World Order" or "The New World Order?" What I mean is this: Is it a single entity wielding powers of illusion, or an all-inclusive private club? Can any qualified person join, and what are the qualifications? Just asking, since the Order is supposed to be steering the financial vessel of the globe to doomland. Another thought that I had is this: How is anybody on this planet going to get enough countries together to agree on the best way to guide the world finances, when those countries can't even have a decent discussion with certain nations on any subject? Maybe they should have called it "A Couple of Different World Orders." What about the title "Two or More World Orders"? What is this nonsense? Sounds like that red state/blue state buffoonery back in 2004 that most Americans were propagandized into accepting and playing along with, while a financial con game was being orchestrated on the other side of the wall on Wall Street.

This world will never be for one currency. I feel that by trying to bring about an issuance of a single world currency, these ritualistic-natured lunatics of the order have by default caused not all but much of the economic malaise that we are witnessing now through sheer stupidity. I approve of diversity in currencies. Too much of the same is boring, and possibly financially dangerous for our planet. These unsuccessful efforts have already destabilized the capital markets. In the very near future, this insight of a harmonious light and shared treasures among the profitable global brotherhood is not going to happen.

For example, take Pakistan and India. I don't think they will be merging currencies anytime soon. What about the United States and Iraq, Afghanistan, Iran, and North Korea? America's future with these countries does not look like a match made in heaven, but rather a match made in hell. Russia and the European Union can't see eye to eye. You can't even get the EU to agree with the EU members. So what world order are we talking about here? It's just like everything else—nothing is what it seems.

Some say that the New World Order's ultimate plan is to reduce the total pollution—and population— of the planet by creating phases of chaos. They will achieve their sadistic goals of billions of people being demolished. This is their spiteful, shallow focus. It's just too bad that these entities could not see the bright side of humanity. Their malevolent shadow deities desire us to be no more. Oh, that's a swell arrangement, as well as depressing. Let's just map out their plans for the sake of conversation anyway. Frankly, they just want to destroy all living things on Earth. That's simple enough. This sounds so Luciferian, so Fabianesque. Everyone left remaining after the major destruction will have to live underground like rats happily ever after. Wow, what a brilliant stroke of genius that is. Who came up with that policy of pain? Didn't anyone object to it? Somebody at the meeting of the drone tricksters had to jump up and say, "This strategy would not be in the country's best interest. We must continue to promote this pattern of insanity at a slow pace." Did all the members just say, "Yes, that's a grand plan. Now that's power and we'll be in complete control. I'm game. Count me in."

I'm sure their families will be thrilled with that master plan for their lives. These brainless wonders are so power hungry that they would even let their loved ones go down for the good of their loser organizational games. So do you really think they give a damn about you or me? If this really is a part of their shortsighted intentions, then help is on the way. By reading this book, you have shown that you are willing to become more informed than the average tellurian. You have already helped yourself and others by scanning for facts. One search at a time is how progress happens.

I know this NWO scenario really sounds like a Dr. Evil cartoon plot, but who could argue with the comparative ideology of this vision? These are mythical mad men and women whom very few see, and even less know of. They exist to cater to the well established. But know this! The order's house of goals is built on precarious swamplands. Suddenly, we may all be are sinking, unexpectedly. Their objectives will also be revealed in other ways. If nothing else, the New World Fathers will experience a soul transgression, which is a big deal. So let's fight the good fight, denizens! Don't become too overly impressed by the bling sting of these vipers.

I just thought of a great idea: Let's not listen to these nut cases of persuasion! We as the rightful citizens of the constitutional republic of the United States need to activate our own plan. We're just like the good citizens in the cartoon that defeated Dr. Evil in the end. We can also win in mundane reality! I will be presenting you with some of my solutions for sabotaging the wicked doctors' plan coming up soon. Be strong. Tick, tick, tick—the clock is running.

The Myth of Money Power

When I was following the developing STDs of the wealth factor in the empire of America, one thing was for sure, or at least it appeared to be. The people at the top of the budgetary totem pole had no clue about a wholesale monetary shift that was evolving on the scene in 2007. The crushing credit crunch was approaching! The great financial freeze was on because of a global disbursement of noninvestment-grade loan instruments. That's just for starters. There was negligence galore! What was most interesting, but not surprising, is that the money market game is dominated by the white race, specifically, white males. I'm not saying this to bring a glare on a certain racial background, but I'm just making an observation from my research. I'm not a racist. I respect all cultures and species of creatures. Besides, my wife is of Caucasian descent. The system classifies me as being black. I'm talking about business now—it's not personal.

I know these facts because I watched those financial shows daily and did not see many minorities, period! The reason I am making this observation is to let those of you who didn't keep a close eye on the scene know that this is the case. You might just take this point for granted. I've seen it with my own eyes while keeping a scope on the men and some women trying to digitize the anatomy of market crash into simple integers.

The process of this predominantly male silhouette of ghost numbers was a feat to behold. Egos congratulating egos. Then the cracks started to appear. Their worst enemy had approached the Wall Street platform, front and center. Credit Default Swaps! No one knew quite sure how to price these garbage real estate CDS derivatives. They dismissed conventional standards and wisdom previously set by the regulators. Talk about the obliteration and overthrow of the stock market. The enforcers themselves fell down on the job. They misled themselves with their highly concocted pedigree of self worth. The system of checks and balances was left unguarded. The keys to the locks that protected the world financial banking vaults were lost forever. The bailout stampede to your savings and checking funds was on! Now you have it! Now you don't!

It's best to clarify my position when it comes to Wall Street and Washington. They both equal 'Wallshington' Street to me. I know I might be overstepping my author's creative privilege with that 'Wallshington' phrase, but cut me a little slack. In most ways these organizations are one and the same today, anyway. One policy affects another. In other words, you wash my dirty laundry and I'll wash yours. I probably watched more of "The Street" shows than most did back in the day. What I saw brought sheer distress in my mind. Day after day I would widen the radius of my financial field glasses and scale the walls of Wall Street. The picture I was receiving while spying NSA style was explicitly clear. The focal point of the stock market joint Wall Street, was nowhere to be seen. Even with a high-powered telescope, you probably could not find someone in charge. Really. A lot of smoke was blowing into the faces of the retail investors and the public, but that's all it was. Smoke and mirrors. I couldn't find a specific focus point in either house. It was simply chaotic. It was like turning to the financial circus channel on the tube. A lot of bright political false declamations in Washington. A ton of dark financial realities on the Street. I knew that the good ol' days of the Dow Jones being at 14,000 was a thing of the past. Probably never to be seen again in our lifetimes.

Looking back on it, there's no way that I could not compare the scenario to an insane asylum, with the CEOs and top talent of multinational corporations screaming, "We are the experts, I want my bonus now!" Not many were awake at the wheel, but that's okay as long as the media has forgiven them. The main media is the mouthpiece for defaulter companies that advertise on the Street. There were many asleep at the wheels that drove this economy off of the cliff. The only problem is that they don't know what has hit them yet. The so-called representatives are as shocked as any of the uninformed sleepwalking cadets today that make up for most of the citizenry in this country and the world at large.

The Wallshington types are the same semi-comatose snap, crackle, and pop characters that were supposed to be guiding this economic craft to safety. We have to make sure that these slickers don't bring us down with them. Maybe, we all might go with them to their piggish extortioners' jails. I hope not. Now, is that enough to make you just shake your head or what? So again I say, what New World Order? We are suffering from a disorder of no romance from our finance. I call this condition "The Green Plague." More on that in the next chapter. All that I can report back is that every company was out for themselves. Even as the ground was shaking, not enough financial leaders used their panoramic view and said, "Look, I think the investment world has been compromised. Let's look into it now before it gets worse." The kleptocracy was trying to save their own wallets first. The little smart guys and gals who worked on Wall Street and Main Street were caught up in the middle. I don't think they knew what pulled the rug from under their employment feet so fast.

The economic TV hosts were also trapped. Do they tell the news the way it is and drag other companies down, or do they lighten up the story about the firm and make the reporting more favorable for investors? You know, the old pretend and extend. In most cases the latter path won out. How do you think we got so deep into this gloomy fog before everyone started screaming? As of this writing, October 2009, the press screaming ain't very loud. Damn! That's sad.

You can't get these folks to agree on the simplest of facts, such as, are we in a recession or not? Is it the Greater Depression? Did the leniency of regulations cause this open wound or not? So how are they, the NWO, going to get every nation's indulgence to agree on a common currency goal for the benefit of all mankind? I can't envision it. Not when it comes to the money. The synthetic power brokers won't take no for an answer. They want it all for themselves. Funny how they could have everything and end up with nothing. So can we. Even the big dogs won't escape this pain of dollar disdain.

Now, some of the creators of this slamdown are pushing their books. I wondered if they are so rich and all-powerful, why do they need to sell a book? Simple answer to that: greed and to rewrite history. It really shows that they just were not up to the task of reining in the spending of one of the greatest economies in the free world.

Out of Cash, Time to Dash

It's all a race to the bottom now. Who gets your dollar first? What crook agency gets to wipe out your bank notes? My theory is that the New World Order can only operate when the economic conditions are favorable to support their hare-brained schemes. From everything that I've read and heard about this NWO fool's paradise, it has a diabolical mission. For them to execute a plan of world government domination, they need to have access to a lot of money to protect their investment interests. Enter the American tax dollars. Also, they have to demonstrate some fanciful image of financial stability to safeguard the confidence of the patrons.

In other words, hide their perilous dealings in clear view under the public's nose. They also must maintain a budget for a highly sophisticated armament detail. Without a security apparatus functioning properly on their behalf, a nation-state of highly developed democratic societies themselves is threatened. What world will the NWO control if the Earth system goes belly up? We only have one that I know of: the one that we exist on. Maybe they have a hidden secret world somewhere that we don't know about yet.

One example of an panoptic organization that demands large amount of funds to operate is the International Monetary Fund, the IMF. As I am winding down this book in the spring of 2010, Greece is defaulting on its debt. The world organizations can't seem to find enough funds to rescue the country. Why would they break their necks to save Greece if they want the world to be destroyed? It's because if Greece goes down then the entire Eurozone will become unstable and create even more disruption in the global economic markets. That is not what they desire. The IMF flew to Greece to try to help them solve their emergency default crisis. That's my point. Even these large bank-type operations cannot deal with the insecurity of nations falling apart. Do you really think that they crave the world to cease existing? Anyone can fail and claim success. The day late and a trillion dollars short crowd just did. They gave everyone the misleading impression that they meant for things to turn out this way, when nothing could be farther from the truth. You hear talk show hosts spread the fear about these organizations' need for despair. The host needs to realize that the causes of our financial losses in many ways are connected to the panic they're spreading about these propaganda pranksters.

You can see this theme played out in any popcorn western's flick all the time. The power over the people must be absolute as far as these phony rat corporations are concerned. "Never let the people get ahead" is their ticket. But always in the westerns, the solid citizens would rise up against the so-called lawmakers, who usually are the lawbreakers. Then some hero cleans the town up and takes no prisoners. At that moment freedom is restored back to the townspeople. Maybe one day in the near future, this empire can be cleaned up, too, with justice fully restored. Then the American public also will once again get that bright vision and feel the sunlight of justice. We deserve it. We must fight for lifting the veil of darkness off of our nation's reputation. This has more to do with who owns your state of being and righteousness: You do!

These folks from the NWO are getting too much credit for being so smart, really they do. I watched and listened to some of the most well-known speaking intellectuals who are on the money circuit. I'm not going to name names, but you would be strikingly impressed by my profile list of the so-called powerful elite. I'm not fazed by it though. Look around. Now we must meet and greet a future cascade of deficit avalanches these characters have caused to pile upon us. I always say, put up or shut up. Remember, this is still just a mundane event. The attack of the humanoids is underway by an unworthy clientele of a cynical nature. A race was on for your cash. You know the garbage that China, Japan, and a few others buy from us as treasury bills, among other financial instruments, and then lend them back to you.

When the going was good you could not find many power broker jokers whose feet were on the ground. They were all living by the code of just dancing blindly until the money music stops. "The money basket is full and we're gonna eat the people's bank accounts alive!" they cheered.

Now that the golden empire's homes are crumbling, and a reduction in the wealth and health of the economy is looking extremely precarious, the power brokers are scrambling. No one is taking the blame for the slowdown. Wall Street will be knee jobbing for a handout soon. Now we will forever be known as the "Bailouts are Us" generation. I say, "Before Wall Street died, they ate us alive!" Now the stock market is so timid that the least bit of bad news can cause major shifts in the market mentality. Just the perception of China indicating that it will no longer buy the U.S. junk debt can take the entire economic system down.

The Credit Crunch Saves the Day

As a matter of fact because of these sidewinding swindlers—and you know who they are—the entire world's financial and political systems have been turned upside down. Their yearning for greed and the temporary fix it delivers for the hardcore financial addicts took us down. I've seen the effects of an imbalanced stock exchange myself. Now, you do also.

There was a time recently when one of the number one conversations on the Internet was that the United States, Mexico, and Canada were going to become one nation. A new currency called the Amero would be the new money, eventually for purposes of buying goods. The whole idea was building steam with the NSA, Homeland Security, the Bush administration, and other agencies. For sure, many said that this is the end game to destroy America's sovereignty. The politicians pushing this agenda were all too satisfied to move forward with this plan at lightning speed. "We got those sucker public peons now!" they shouted. "Beg for mercy, you underdogs!" Just then, a wall of justice came to the good peoples' defense in some strange way in 2007. The credit crunch hit and the believers of the New World Order fantasy had to face reality. The stock market was in massive trouble. The investment into their plans of pretense about the Amero currency was falling apart faster than a jackrabbit trying to escape a coyote party. The jig was up!

They had to fade to black on the false front of imperialism. Their dreams had decayed into ashes because of a double-faceted defeat. First, the plan was disingenuous; next, and most importantly, the very lifeblood of any crazy scheme is money, and when the markets froze from the credit crunch, so did their maniacal misjudgments. Little did they realize that the very tactics they were trying to implement needed a systematic process of regularity, just the same as the stock market did. Trying to execute their underhanded pretense was unfaithful to a policy of order. That was a major mistake. Their plan was doomed from the start. Just as everything else they ventured to accomplish had failed. That's your New World Order of lower intelligence working against you.

In some ways, the federalists did get their promise of power, but it's a perverted outcome. The system might still go to the Amero currency out of necessity following the collapse of a failed dollar. There's no other placeholder for the dollar, but that was not Plan A. This proves my point. No order or system can defeat the universal laws. No counterfeit plotting schemes can surpass the measure of having basic, honest economic fundamentals. A market must have integrity if it's to have a foundation to stand on, or it's going to fall. Until any New World Order honors the golden rules, not one of these conglomerates will survive ... including the sweet-talking tricksters who present us with these hazardous misfortunes that await us today.

No thanks to these skunks for their legendary blunders. If the NSA had perhaps spied on Wall Street and the White House dealings, we would not be in this predicament. Oh sorry, I had a senior moment. They can't spy on the White House and Wall Street. That allegedly would prove collusion on their part. It took a credit crunch to take the sizzle out of their razzle-dazzle plans. Now in this special case, I will propose a salute: Viva la Credit Crunch! Yeah, I said it. Only because it might have postponed or canceled even more financial human suffering.

Shadow Banking Is Tanking

Let me come at the shadow banking system, the mammoth covert operation from a strange perspective. Once again let me state that while during my research, a pattern emerged which looks as if real estate is the only industry that can finance a military as gigantic as the United States'. So you need a lot more cash to fund this money-puking germ war virus. A country requires an endless amount of legal tender in its furnaces to keep the fire of puzzlement for the service people carrying forward. One way to acquire those kinds of bucks is to show the taxpayer one set of numbers and to disguise a private funding program off the books for important black missions. The black government organizations used front companies, or banks that you can seal a classified document label on, and withhold the truth that any of the illicit businesses exists. They just claim state secret as a defense. So poli-typical.

In following this substantial momentous monetary and housing collapse event since 2006, I feel that this is not an economic downturn, but an economic crooked turn! Now that I got that off my chest, let me continue on with my current thought flow. As I was verbalizing in the back of my mind's calculator, I wondered just where all of the commerce for the so-called black programs funding could be coming from. Even before I became an observer of Wall Street, I always had a foresight, a focused vision of this mystery. Was Congress approving funds for the secret programs, or did the operations have their own banks? Just where the hell is the money coming from to continue this camouflaged mystery that has been going on for decades? This is all connected to the vindictive New World Order. They are one and the same. One thing's for sure, they both need money to survive, like humans need water to live.

So where does all their money comes from? I know a lot of the diñeros came from the big multinational banks. And I was under the impression that I had heard just about all of the names of most of the largest banks and real estate lenders in the country, just by following the banking industry intently for over three years. You know who they are. The Goldman Sachs, JP Morgan Chase types, Citibank, and so forth. Was I in for a shocking surprise! I mean, I followed the credit default swaps, the subprime collapse, the stimulus package insanity, the bankrupt corporations galore, and many of these instigators of the green dollars plots.

Just when I thought I had a handle on the situation somewhat, some of the worst characters started to rise up from the bottom-dwelling sludge of Wall Street—the black ops banks, in my opinion. In my eyes you can only comprehend this cliffhanger and head-banger to a limited extinct. Trying to get your mind around this whole fiasco only prolongs the agony if you don't know what you're looking for.

For example, there was a major court bankruptcy case involving a corporate giant. Well, the case was so complicated and beyond the jurors' knowledge of corporate fiscal legal affairs that the case was dismissed by the judge because the jurors were so uneducated about the financial facts.

Moving on, there are others that know more about this event than me, but there are plenty of others that know more than about this economic happening. The realization that the banking model that these scam firms use was frivolous at the least, and criminal at worst. Here's the layout. One banking model goes something like the following. The bank only processes home and commercial loans. The more loans they receive from their parent loan company to process, the greater are the fees that they can collect. Can you believe that this racket is called an investment bank? No depositors. It's a front company. They needed loan fees just to stay in business, so they couldn't care less if the loans were legit or not.

Now, here's the important part. They took these loans and packaged them together, and spread them all over the world. Hence, "The Green Plague." They could not resist the temporary gain they would derive from the fees of these contagious toxic debt bombs. Now, just to attempt to simplify this topic in a nutshell is a big job. I'm trying to give you a plain understanding so that the masses can make sense of the layout and get a clearer picture of the secret banks questionable plan of actions.

For a great example of this, let's just use the name, Space Bank. Now this so-called counting house, which is or was the largest commercial lender in the world, was created just in 2006 as a result of a default of a parent company. Say that Space Bank became an offshoot company handling a large amount of real estate loans for their parent company. Let's just ignore the fact that the Space Bank was getting kickbacks from their parent company for the loans they processed. In other words, double pay to play. Fees and kickbacks were the way of the day. The getting was good, but never has the deceit gone so awry. The critical point is that it is so easy to rip off the American imperial gimmick economy. It's been proven time and time again. These investment banks had little to no oversight. They were just running berserk and funneling money to feed their agendas. Because of the dereliction of checks and inspections were passed over, no one will or can ever really discover where all the bank notes went. Once again, the public is not informed enough to interpret these methods of wrongdoing. The boatloads of money for the shadow governments had to come from somewhere. Yeah! The U.S. taxpayers' accounts, never to be repaid!

When I first started hearing about the big dogs in the banking system, I had a bing! bing! moment. I was devoted to tracking this market beast from 2006 to 2009, and never heard of these grand institutions. Recently they revealed themselves to the public in the fall of '09. They were buried deep in the intestines of the financial guts of Wall Street, like a cancer. I'm still trying to determine just what the underworld cartels are claiming as their triumphant manifest destiny. To break it down, from what I can see, if the soon-to-be financial dropoff had not occurred, then these enterprising global syndicates might have never came into the light of day.

The crux of my theory is that whenever an empire has its most immoral, contemptible, and scurviest businesses hidden from public view, then that is probably where the big, kinky, dirty secrets are being deployed. If this once-in-a-lifetime deleveraging breakdown was ever to make these multi-national banks surface to the top of the news, now is the time. We all should start shaking in our boots about right now! A real hyper-havoc could be coming to a town near you. Soon! The status quo is no more. At least these shadow banks are going extinct. How does that song in The Wizard of Oz go? I'll make up my own lyrics: "Ding Dong, the wicked rich are dead!"

Who Missed the Beginning of the Recession?

I feel kind of sorry for the folks who were working in corporate careers and missed the entire recession, along with anybody else, for that matter. I don't know if I have stated this before, but I lived through that heartbreaker of a fiscal flats. Oh yeah, even if you missed it you will still feel the ill effects of the events that have already transpired. If the politicians, economic experts, business people, and citizens had actually lived through the complete recession, their total life preferences would have changed for better or worse, like mine did. It's a force feeding that's going on now.

So much information is floating around that most people don't know where to turn. I feel their pain. Imagine how different our planet would be right now if the proverbial can of commerce didn't just keep getting kicked down the road of illusionary bankrolls. If they had lived through the beginning of that bunch of crap that I suffered through, perhaps they would have regarded the value of the country's financial freedom enough to not let the leadership choke themselves on crimes until they were fat and happy.

In a time-travel concept of daydreaming, I wish we could warp time and revisit an era a few years ago, but only with our current mindset of today. The old adage, "Hindsight is 20/20" is the word of the day. I wish the leaders and the people could go back to the years of 2007-2008 and consciously experience the actual credit crunch and recession while it was in motion. You will witness that these same monetary leaders who became newsworthy back then were lost. It was public knowledge that they flat out missed the complete beginning year of the recession. Not a clue that the recession had arrived and jolted the world's superpower into its current prehistoric financial direction.

The way I feel about the economic experts who missed the recession is this: If you missed the initial year, then just shut up and go away! If you didn't notice a major financial departure before, how can you be trusted to get the next call correct? You have no voice when you were right there in the economic soup daily, and missed this pivotal moment in American economic history. If you missed the credit crunch of 2007, the stock market crash of 2008, the recession of 2008 through 2009, the Greater Depression and the global financial collapse of 2010 and soon-to-be 2011, then go sit down somewhere and let the grown folks handle this monster problem that some screwups created.

Wall Street has fallen and they can't get up. They felt no wrong could ever happen to the housing market during those times. So trying to get the bureaucracy to look forward as to what might be coming down the tracks ahead was a non starter conversation. The watering hole's financial charts at the Wall Street bar were always characterized as a forward-looking indicator. Year after year everyone just assumed that this is the case. The market would always rebound. We all understood that there will always be minor reversals in the market. This was the prevailing thought at this point in time.

Then the management changed on the Street and the economy expanded. The slogan became, "Drink up, good stockateers, we are rich now. For the price of a glass of "scampagne" you too can feel like a fat-cat fiscal fantasy. So I drank up, looked forward with these economic suspects, moved forward and straight ahead, and then fell off Wall Street's bar stool ... along with everyone else who thought they were in good standing financially everywhere around the world. This was the happy hour of transgression. On second thought, let's not drink to that. I should have known that sooner or later we all would have to suck up austerity's drink of choice. Economic Pain with a cherry on top! Now I have a splitting hangover from watching my bank account getting watered down to emptiness. The phony financial bootlegging operation got me again!

While investigating the hip-hip-hoorays and the slaps on the backs for the Wall Street executives, I observed that the rich got richer. Then I had a distant visionary moment, what some might call a flashback activation. I saw a time when the stock exchange floors were packed with people working everywhere. Not a ghost town like it is today. The greed factor helped to create an absence of personnel on the floor for sure. Let's please hope that these wannabe decision-making tycoons are not the same ones in charge of putting this economic Humpty Dumpty back together again. Unfortunately, they are.

Will the NWO Achieve Their Dreams?

You might be wondering what all of this insight has to do with the present moment. Everything, and the New World Order. Think about the phrase, New World Order, for a flash, because that's all it deserves is a flash for these flakes. So I ask of you, what New World is the Order going to be ordering around? Certainly not this one. This sphere of creation is in grave jeopardy of decay, because of these world order types. So you tell me, are they going to do as an exceptional economic job the next time as they have this time around?

Tell me, what is it exactly that we have to look forward to from their lame brain strategies? Will the farters be teeming with other ingenious minds the next time they are in charge? So, are they in charge now? Let's give credit where credit is due. If they are in charge of the world as many seem to believe in that idea, we need a new life order just to escape from these nutcases. Is this a Satan setup or what? Throw the politicians and bankers enough rope, and they will hang themselves ... and us along with them.

These people are spiritual and mental slackers. What good are all the Illuminati conspiracies if they can't save the world? What good is the church, if they can't save the world? What good is a political system, if it is the very reason that the world as we know it is in danger of disappearing? To believe in these cliques to save humanity, you might as well call on Santa Claus to help get us out of this jam. All of these groups can be worthless to the soul of a nation if they let the best part of your life slip away.

As a matter of fact, because of their infectious nature, the genius of the public has been stripped away like an old man losing his teeth. That's it. The empire has no clothes and no teeth. America has no triple-A ratings on their bonds. The dollar, treasuries, and homes also have not maintained their value very well. You think? "Calm down!" I say to myself. Remember, we're just living through Bush's third term. Picking up the pieces.

Either these characters have decided to let us as a society walk the final plank of life blindfolded, or they don't know what is up any more than do the animals at the zoo. Sorry, I didn't mean to insult the animals. The animals know better than we ever could dream of knowing. Maybe we should just call this epic "The Great Equalizer." Now the rich are becoming the poor. Welcome to our world. "We ain't never had much, and now you'll know how it is to live a life of survival and adaptation." You see when you set into motion a system of unfairness, it gives a distinct advantage to the few over the many by stealing from the poor and giving to the rich. This never works. Then a wicked destabilizing deteriorating game has been instantly activated upon humanity and we all lose. All inclusiveness is the only way for any nation to survive.

My last statement on the NWO is this. I told you I had a few things to say about these infamous home wreckers. What really are these globalist goals, anyway? Is it to take down the planet and all living things on it? If this is so, then are they getting closer to destroying every living creature's right to life that the good Creator has bestowed upon them as a gift? Who is the globalist God anyway? Do they have a spiritual purpose of contribution for all mankind? If not, why are people giving their power away to these lost souls anyway? Are there penalties for crimes against the galactic bodies of universal laws? Since these invaders had no part in creating the universe, who are they to attempt to suspend the eternal laws of creation because of their puny egotistical desires? It really comes down to the will of the citizens to wake up. It's time to become aware and know that we hold the power pieces on the chessboard of our lives. We are divine beings! Anyone who debates this point has much more wisdom to acquire. Instead of debating as to whether we are divine or not, that time could be better used by discovering your gifts and using them to help others who have troubles. I will express my views on this point in depth in a later chapter.

Just to prove a point, let's use the rock, paper, and scissors game for an analogy. Remember that old game. Say that the New World Order is the rock that always breaks the people, which are the scissors. As long as the community stays unconscious and subservient to the rock, they will continue to obey every threat of fear that the rock is promising to bring daily. If this is so, then the citizens might as well scream "Uncle! Uncle!" and raise their white flags of surrender. To create a defense against the rock of fear, the scissor people could raise their consciousness to achieve their victory. They could become more informed about how to elevate their minds to visualize themselves transforming into the paper. If achieved, that process would allow the underdogs to become paper and cover the powerless rock. No longer would the solid patrons be subject to the trickery of the stone, and they would defeat the deceit. It's worth a shot.

Take any so-called NWO figure and research them, whether they be man or woman, and I can just about assure you that they are even more concerned about the world economy than you or I. Well, not me. They have more to lose. We are the folks who have worked hard for a living, swimming upstream against the economic tide. We didn't have much on the material side of life any-way, but we were okay with that. These world-order bush leaguers, if there is such a body, are looking out for number one and screw the rest. It's human nature. That's how we ended up in this jam of doom.

Know this, from the beginning of this chapter, my entire thesis has been that when money is tight, everywhere in the world, corporate greed systems start to break down. These politicians could not give a damn about controlling the world when there's no profit to be made from it. So why do it? Even now, money follows growth opportunities. It doesn't matter what the name of the country or business is. There is no loyalty to any nation-state. Money has no heart.

For some reason the big-wig bankers and lawbreakers have forgotten that they also have to live on this decaying Earth rock. I've heard about the many theories about a secret space program for the elite migrating to other worlds in the solar system. Just a few questions that I have about this plan. First, what assurances do they have that after they help destroy the planet Earth that they would be safe anywhere else that life exists? These characters would be worse than war criminals. What's below that? If a common bank robber must pay for crimes against a certain bank, then why would there be no Karmic retribution for the New World Order robbing an entire world? So you tell me, who is it that would board this ship with these immoral crooks into outer space? That sounds like a winner. Not! What a safe and victorious journey that would be, right? Just trying to strike a little balance and sanity in the scenario. You'd have to be an idiot to get on board. For sure, you would trust your life's eternal future with some shady villains, to say the least. Now, don't you feel free from danger escaping with the dishonest misfits, whether they be man or ancient aliens.

Where is it written that their will is the way and this must be so? Some will do anything for a buck. Also, what guarantees do these duck-and-cover sidesteppers have that their soul plan is a work of perfection and protection for the saviors of these sick souls? What's going to stop these monsters from destroying their next land of inhabitation? I, for one, would not want to be aboard their one-of-a-kind spacecraft. They have already caused plenty of hell on this spacecraft we call Earth. Would you leave with them? The evil is not the environment that they exist in, but in their petty, warped minds. Then again, I wonder whether the last Great Depression was caused by the same organizations that caused this one? Of course, some of them were there. We must stop the evil empires. Their deception must not be allowed to alter our perception and life direction.

Against All Odds

The elite seems more to me every day like some kind of special needs charity event, coordinated by the graduates of the school. The tribulations that we are going through now feel like some big economic promotions full of joy. Yippee! Not! These lowdown folks operate in the ego. They can be defeated. Control is their goal, and that shows their weakness of soul. It is well known that control is an alter ego action of the objective state of mind. According to the universal laws, the objective state of mind is the lowest level of consciousness. Do these so-called clandestine types of imaginary power have security forces to protect them? If not, then where does their power base get its authority from? Does their influence lie just with the movement of electronic bank promissory notes? Who enforces the rules that are executed? If they do not have enforcers to fulfill their laws, then they are totally vulnerable and can be overtaken.

So, these spiritually inept shysters are not ones to fear if you have a heart of wisdom. If the elitists were morally advanced, domination of the world would be of less importance to their well being, anyway. That goes for any national leaders, too. Love and harmony always conquers fear. It has to. There will always be more good in the world than bad. Even with the lame invasions and occupations. There are still more good people in the world than sinners.

If this is not so and the perceived notion of elite clan are correct, we will all soon perish because of their diabolical motives anyway. Then, why obey their current laws that are restricting us from our true heritage today. Just say, "The Hell with you and the Heaven within me." Regain your natural birthrights and powers granted to you by a higher, principled Creator. We've got to take the huff and puff out of these delusional folks' persona. We must bring out the "Big Bad Wolf" syndrome that really describes them.

These world order types are not supernatural beings. They can't control their own lives, much less your life. They came to earth for the same reasons you did: to learn the lessons of life. They think they are as grand as the universal principles. Obviously, they do. They are the ones who need to be scared. Our life trip is temporary. The next life of transformation is where we pay our debts for misdeeds in this life cycle, or move in a higher purpose with the all-knowing Creator force. Is there anyone of you who would trade places with these politicians and the globalists at the so-called pearly gates of Heaven? I don't see any volunteers. They don't have some kind of God card in their possession that promises them eternal life from punishment of their crimes. They don't get to decide just when their time of death arrives on their doorstep, so why do they get to dictate when your spiritual reunion with your Maker begins? They came out of some woman's body cavity, same as you, and their flesh will return to ashes as this cycle of life requires. Even if they are reptilians from other worlds as some suggest, they have a Creator of laws to adhere to, also. No world gets a free ride. Your death is yours alone with your Creator. Don't leave it up to others to decide. The only way that happens is when you give up your power and rights to the lesser beings of the dark forces of ignorance.

I'm just trying to take some of the shine off their coat of armor. There's got to be some way that we as honest people can come out on top of this challenge from the weak ones of the Order. Our Creator God would not leave us without answers to the deeds and questions necessary to handle and use our might to battle the evil that these incompetent hegemonies of perceived prestige have planned for us. Question not a man until you have examined his actions and found them sinful. When you are fighting for the right, you always have a chance for things to turn out positive. We have the kids, the animals, and nature on our side. All we need to do is raise the courage of our own spiritual genius within, which fortifies our position and shields us from the worst that these parasites have to offer us. Our zest for a continuation of the human condition will improve dramatically regardless of what any negative nutcases try to implement. As long as your heart is in a good place, it does not matter what physical place of containment the body is placed.

These entities are weaklings. I can't understand why these organizations are so glorified. If these psychos break up the world enterprise and destroy a wonderful life system experiment, then how will they survive? In order for their plot to be successful, there would have to be no counterbalance mechanisms in the order of Creation to combat their ominous yearnings. All ancient wisdom teaches that this is not so, and can't be accepted as a fact of life. When you live in the physical world, this is how things can go wrong. That is why the ancient knowledge taught lessons about not admiring the body. Harmony can only be achieved by the many that will not be deceived.

Besides, these special needs, kleptomaniac, World Order types must have a way for people to buy their products. That's like a business owner burning down their own place of employment, only to realize later that now they have no way to earn an income. Sounds like these spiritual neophytes plans. Look at all the businesses that these jokers were allowed to scorch at home and abroad.

Lately, a more appalling focus has come to mind about the direction of the phantom organizations. I had to ask myself the question, what if no World Order folks had a clue, which I'm convinced they don't, about the timing of the crash and were not in position to not only save themselves or their families, but also they could not have the time or the vision to even consider being in power at the time of the economic demise? Then that would be a much more alarming and daunting task for the nations and the world to correct anytime soon. In other words, you are totally on your own.

Nowadays it seems as though the lame brains did not really want our liberties after all. They are on the run trying to protect their own posteriors now. You should see the bodyguards assigned to these folks. I guess they may not be worried about your puny little life, but they sure are concerned about staying the course as far as keeping them alive. There are not enough laws to protect anyone as long as these slimeballs are calling the shots. The unlawfulness on steroids of the entire breakdown kicks into some other dimension that the world has never experienced before with these believers in charge. It would definitely be lights out for millions, including the New World Order clan. I've heard all the talk that the world leaders would have to be taken to underground bunkers for future preservation of the government system. Some of these officials are not worth saving. I ask myself many times, what guarantees are there that under the earth is so safe? If a hyperquake rips through that bunker, I would not want to be in there. Also, who is going to make the call to go down under? That's not an easy call to make. Any second could change life forever.

We have only one source of security, and that's spiritual soul security. That is why it was important for these leaders to not sell their souls in the first place. No one could stop them from selling out, and they sold us down the golden river. What about the world leaders who are not members of the so-called New World Order? Will they be allowed to live? Will they be on the run like everyone else? I would hate to be a politician during this era, because the masses are going to blame the system for their miseries. Check in on the Iceland meltdown. Chaos could be just around the corner for the U.S. soon. This ain't no freakin' movie; I've seen the writing on the banking loan contracts that led us to these disillusions of financial decomposition.

As a result of all the crony games, now the greatest empire in modern times went from being a superpower, to soon becoming a banana republic in just eight short years. This is perhaps the most dramatic event in the history of the financial world. To witness a superpower that has ruled the world for over 200 years, only to be demoted to a third world country in eight short years is mystifying. How could this have happened to America as a sovereign nation? Well, in my opinion, the world order rats have been eating away at this country's democratic laws and funds for many decades. The American politicos sold this union out many moons ago. So, when the roof caved in during the 2007, many insiders were not surprised. As a matter of fact, we were surprised it didn't happen sooner than then. Well, that's your country's leaders for you. Ready to sell out for a copper penny. Any one of them.

They, we, and our ancestors ended up with nothing, a big fat zero for building a jewel of a nation.

So, when people speak about some ghastly NWO, as if it were some kind of privileged organization, I say, please don't fear, look at the little men and women behind the curtain of deception. Look, there's no one there. They all left the shop to prepare for the coming disorder they created. That's bleedership for you. When the going gets tough, the leaders run the other way. They are only human ... right? If they do have only evil in their hearts, we might know soon. The Wall Street bar and grill is serving a special meal of reptile default tonight. The waiter asks a citizen customer, "Would you like a little reptilian dish tonight, sir? It's being served right now with economic golden eggs with yokes for dopes."

Silence of the Free Market System

Who knew this country was endowed with so many elites who were enthusiastic student interns in the mortuary business? These folks create graves wherever and whenever they appear. I'm sure that they were rewarded handsomely. Something that frightens me even more is the fact that there will never be another free market capitalistic systems in our lifetime. The empire's financial schemes are all cadavers. Send them to the deep blue caves. Case closed. We need a newly updated model of financial systems.

I ask the New World Order cast, are you happy now? This was the plan, right? To bring America to its knees. Wall Street is a skeleton of its former identity. The global economic outlook is even more inauspicious. Is this proof of the disappearance of America as an individual nation and independent state or what? What government in its right mind would sell its nation's rights for such a cheap price to a bunch of branded and stamped all-inclusive buddy-buddy worldwide clan? Here's the kicker. They never had to sell the federation in the first place. They have always been in control of its destiny.

The most horrifying fact of all is that these same people are in charge of the command of this nation and can order the use of a nuclear weapon. Also, they can order the use of martial law in any city. The justice has been so compromised by the last administration that America has truly lost its moral compass. How will they bring forth justice for the nation when their people have major conflicts within their business models? There aren't many places we can turn to on a national level. The much-discussed NWO money gods can start a crisis, but do they have the power to stop a disaster. These characters don't rate a new rope with me. Like the soul singer, brother James Brown said, "It's better to die on your feet, than to live on your knees." Well, the bright spot is at least you'll know where to place some of the blame for this fiasco. The New World Farters, I mean, Order.

VI
THE GREEN PLAGUE

THERE WAS A CONTAGIOUS financial virus that metastasized across the planet in the summer of 2007. I caught it early on, and now you have it too ... whether you realize it or not. That feeling of sickness that comes from a disease is contaminating every financial instrument in reach and in sight. Only this time, it was created in some obscure institutional laboratory called Wall Street, funded by the Federal Reserve Bank, Washington politics, and lobbyist policies galore! At first I questioned whether this detrimental dollar disease was hereditary. Was I born with it, or did I catch this virus from close contact with others in the financial markets? I'm speaking about the infamous "Green Plague!" A failed capital investment plot that reduced the dominant international currency, the dollar, to a level of insignificance and swept the world like no other dark economic epidemic on record. What is it, you might ask.

Well, that is the question for the ages. I coined the catchphrase, the Green Plague, from my observation of Wall Street in my watcher's laboratory. I noticed a tremendous amount of incoming junk derivatives causing a disruptive force of contagion in the national and global stock markets. Eventually I realized that we had been eaten alive from the inside out by some man-manipulated money infection. The citizens had no awareness of these silent but deadly pathogens of credit default swaps, an illness that had infiltrated the bloodstreams of our wealth existence. By this time, my lens of vision became clearer in my microscope of the sys-tematic invasion of a germ that we were not born with or inherited.

Something on planet Earth blew up and sent the economic fundamentals to the galactic stratosphere, never to return to normalcy again. There were money meteors falling from the unpredictable cauldrons of the galaxies with new diseases. A meteor filled with a storm of microorganisms unknown to the human race from the skies of an attacking monetary federal finance space system. What happened to the stock market was like something from another planet struck us where it hurts, but sadly this is not the case. This consequential sickness of finance is unfortunately caused by mankind's deviations from fiscal sanity. This viral bug that attacked our planet came from the terrestrial minds. We could not have imagined this to happen in our lifetime, our children's generations or even your pets. They say a cat has nine lives. Well, with this budget-busting bug spreading at such a rapid rate, we may not approach the standard of living that we were used to again ... even if we live as long as that cat. We also know that cats can die if they are not careful. The same goes for the human animal.

The Vikings' Egos

This outbreak of the Green Plague makes the swine flu and any other kind of virus look like a preschool picnic at the lake. Why? Never before has the ego-driven human caused so much self-destruction among and upon themselves in history. Here's an old wives' tale. The Vikings of long ago had a similar crossroad to ponder. While coming to a new land, they didn't know how they were going to survive the fierce winters. So a native tribe paid the Vikings a visit to give them some advice for living in this land during the heavy snows. Well, the Vikings told these native Indians of the land to not insult their higher intelligence. They were the mighty Vikings, and no little brown people were going to tell them anything about survival. They told them that they "look like brown monkeys and couldn't know more than the Super Vikes." Well, to this day the native tribe is still living thousands of years later, and the Vikings vanished shortly after that first encounter. The moral of the story is that the ego alone can cause an extinction event all by itself.

The Creators of the Subprime Slime Crime

Nothing is too large or small for the creators of this deadly affliction to desire and destroy, when it comes to them getting richer and hoarding the jewels of a nation and its people. Raping us and robbing the treasury of all they come in contact with. What kind of a person would do to this to the world and sleep soundly at night? Thank your lucky stars they have to sleep some time, or these scoundrels would be able to heap even more damage, if you could possibly imagine more torment on the people could be invented in their monetary labs. Will the real bank robbers please stand up? Suddenly Wall Street is silent, empty, and on the phones with their partners in crime, the White House. The regulators are nowhere to be found. Massive laws are being broken. It's party time. Yippee!

There are no consequences, the big bad wolves proclaim! They were making so much loot by gouging the people and spreading their commercial packages of collapse around the world, what could possibly be wrong with this strategy? "Besides, who cares? Let the poor public suckers suffer, and one day, they will gain their wealth back that we stole from them. Right now, tell them the economic seas are calm and there's no need to panic." Little did they know that the filth they moved around the world would also become a pandemic in their own evil minds and lives. They will lose their loot and maybe a lot more in the times ahead.

Now, don't misunderstand me, most of the gentlemen and ladies involved in finance were not invited to these laboratory experiments. Only the power shakers, the big crooks wore the high security clearance badges on their lab coats in order to gain permission to enter and conduct secretive scientific manipulation of the market disorderliness. Their modus operandi was to cause the self-destruction of the integrity of a method of finance that was already deformed to begin with. They wanted to create a process of digress.

The middle class is now confronting a horrifying outlook as these lab experiments from these green money scientists have gone terribly wrong. They created a "clone-onic" defective model that resembled a stock market. Just enough to recognize and keep the people calm. Still to this day, it is like this: "Got a house to sell you that's upside down. Great price!" It's only going down 50% this year. Better jump on it now. Sounds like I work for the networks. What's a plague-ridden man to do?

My Own Diagnosis

Let me describe the appearance and diagnosis of this elementary-level gimmick as it happened to me. Most have not felt the condition to the extent I have for obvious reasons. One diagnosis I discovered in my own lab is the groundwork for what would be known the world over as the Green Plague. A systematic damaging macroorganism that I knew would infect the planet, but while working on this problem, I did not know that I also became infected. As I studied this pathogen of greed, it was transmitted through the immunological disorder of my financial accounts. I became stressed out over my future funds. I saw my funds getting set on fire in the dark laboratory of green bacterium, Wall Street. I became very ill daily, wavering, frightened, unsure, and exhausted. My whole existence suddenly became about beating this monetary disorder and still maintaining a financially surviving household.

In the first stage of this plague I became disillusioned. I noticed it had metastasized in my entire being by eating away at my mind, body, and soul. At some point through the years of chasing this crash, I realized that this decrepit business monster organism had impaired the fiscal vision of most economic experts, and the blind were persuading the blind. Now, so many folks are going blind from this plague. They, too, got eaten up by the setup of penny-ante crimes. There's no way for them not to get the Green Plague of the subprime slime crime.

The Decoupling Fiction

Wait, I know just the cure for what ails the world's money disease. It's a remedy the old folks talked about a long time ago, since the time of the last great depression. It's called decoupling. Of course, I'm being facetious now. A short description of decoupling is basically when a Nation State becomes independent from the global economy and funds their own society through alternative methods of currencies. They can dissolve their relationship with some international partners and keep others. In other words, tell the countries that are not in sound financial health that you were disconnected from the global network of capital with no regard for your well-being. You must go at it alone. So basically, places such as China, India, or Russia are telling the United States that because you wrecked the system of wealth, the world no longer requires your services.

The only catch with this unimaginable concept is that America may be the most powerful corruption machine the world has ever seen, and has spread the Green Plague of wealth death in every corner of the earth. Still, any nation that wants to perform capitalistic business on a grand scale has to do business with the United States of Zimbabwe. Sorry for the blunder. I mean, they must deal with the United States of America! This is the reason why I've written these alleged financial facts.

At the time when all of this breakaway from the U.S. conversation was in a heated debate in 2007, TV hosts were screaming that they love that global story. (Remember Dubai.) The Internet was blowing up on the possibility that the free market world can exist without the superpower, the United States of America. That all came back down to Earth quick, fast, and in a hurry when the plain facts about the numbers concerning the GDP of every nation resurfaced. GDP stands for the Gross Domestic Product of a country. These numbers brought a sense of humbleness to the picture. Here's why.

When the discussion of decoupling was at its peak in 2007-08, the economies were grooving along. The misdirection play was in full effect mode. The false financial bankrolling was seemingly still on fire. American consumers during that business cycle accounted for over $9.3 trillion in global domestic product of world GDP. Here's the shocker! Mind you, this was when every country was making money hand over your bank account. The country with the next closest GDP to the U.S. consumers was China, with a total of $1.2 trillion of the world's GDP, and then India, at just under $1 trillion. So you see, even with all the billions and billions of people in these nations, they cannot even begin to replace the American consumers' buying power. We account for 70% of America's spending. So the picture is clear—forget about the decoupling theory coming to save the day. So goes the U.S. empire, so goes the world! I'm hearing a song worm in my head again. I think it's by the rock group from the 70s group Sugarloaf. The song is called "Green Plague Lady." Actually, the song was called "Green-Eyed Lady." Welcome to the land of dreams into nightmares.

Make the Rules As You Go

Welcome to the spaghetti finances of Eddy Fast Hands. The fastest hands in the money data game are not just made with a Wall Street computer, but also with the White House ballpoint pen, which is quicker than the eye. So many rule changes happened in 2008 that I became dizzy. So did the market. I can never state enough how many times that I heard that phrase from commentators, that the market hated uncertainty. Well, it's too late for that! That's the least of our problems. You should have thought about that before all this jive jinx started. If we could change our personal banking accounting rules the way these corporations do, then we could really have a party.

When you really think about it, the broadness of the market is so grand that no one can really keep up with who's doing the wrong things that's affecting everyone else and when. How would you know? This whole green sludge fund of financial voodoo took on a life of its own. No one could stop it from growing into a mass stupidity of digits. There's a certain downer vibration that coincides with the breakdown of a worldwide financial system. The rules are nonexistent. Make them up as you go. We have approached the territory of the insane in the membrane!

At this step in my evolution I am not the same as I used to be. Once this misery gets inside of you, there's a letdown. There has been a DNA transformation within my existence. Oh, I'm still connected to our planet, always. Even before all this chaos exploded, my motto has consistently been: Always keep one foot on planet and one foot off. What I mean by this is: I never have been the kind of person to just believe in what I can see, hear, touch, and feel, as was taught in our schooling. I've always marched to a different drummer. I know that the unseen world is the seen world. Why do you think I am writing this book? Only because I had the insight to pick up on a vibration of abnormality in my intuition and I paid close attention to it. That being said, here I am today still walking around with this Green Plague inside of me and living to tell about. Oh, one day everyone will become aware of their misfortune.

Generally speaking, most people just want to go to work earn a paycheck for an honest day of work and go home. Who could understand this pump-and-dump junk anyway? Even with as much of this crap as I have observed, I still can't interpret the game. Who would want to? You can have it. Take over from here for me. You're welcome to. The experts can't even keep up with the speed of this money monster, much less an economic commoner like myself. Many rules that were around in 2007 are not even on the books anymore.

I don't know if you could find anyone in the world who really knows what the rules of the stock market are anymore. Certainly not the politicians. If they did understand it, you can't tell by looking around at the subsidized scene today. You would never know it. It's like watching any professional sporting event these days. Who knows what all the rules are anymore? They are constantly morphing into other meanings. As time shifts, so do the regulations. If you do find someone who claims to know what the laws of the global financial system are, tell them I say good luck in trying to explain them to the sovereign folks!

You Could Catch It, Too

Millions have caught the viral strain of this syndrome, feeling depressed, shameful of their living conditions, no outlook to earn an income, homeless looking for a way to just feed themselves and their family, including pets. The malady of poor health, physically, mentally, and spiritually. Well, I can testify that one of the techniques that I use to help me remain vibrant as a member of this wacky species is to journey into the depths of my soul through spiritual meditation. It's the main remedy that I use to combat this devastating bug. That's just me.

Everybody will have to find their own ways to peace. If you have lost the material gain acquired from earlier in your life, it is not destined for your future lifestyle. Move on and try new things in life. My distant walks in nature with Lori also quiet my mind so that I may receive answers to my greatest concerns in my life. How to deal with the all encompassing Green Plague? I got bit by the bug early in the process but I'm fighting it with all my might.

Another way that helps me to fight it is by telling as many people as I can about it. Hence me writing this book. I'm sorry for the folks who missed the beginning of the recession/depression because it was a grandstanding wallop. You can read about it now, but to experience it was out of this world. I did, and I'm still paying for it now. While I'm penning my book, this information just flows out of me as I battle this disease. My body is feeble in some ways and functioning properly in others. That's what this condition does to you. I am a man who has morning sickness some days, and other days I can get out bed rather easily. I took a hit on this one. A blow to the gut, then the ill health engulfed me. When I write using medical terms about a failed commerce system, I'm writing metaphorically, of course. Yes, I guess we all got some green in us now. I ain't talking about little green aliens and I ain't rapping about greening of the planet, although that is of the utmost importance. What I'm conversing about is the Green Plague, the economic convulsions rapidly consuming every financial cellular structure and everybody in sight.

We've Been Sold Out!

America will never be a free market capital system again. I have serious doubts that it ever was in the first place. Ain't deleveraging of the largest financial system in history just a bunch of fun? The bigger they are, the harder they fall. Understand this, people. If you don't get any other point out of this book, please get this. I don't think anyone else has brought this to the attention of the media or the masses. The pain and strain that humanity is crying about right now is a deleveraging event we are witnessing of biblical proportions. Let's break this down for the common folk: They sold our asses out!

To create this magnitude and intensity of green dollar G-force dropout, there must have been legal tender paper debt plastered all over the walls of Wall Street. The Federal Reserve printing press has seemingly been working overtime for eons, at least the federal economic results of today seems to indicate this. The printing press action of a couple of years ago was cranking out the dough like a high-priced bookie operation in Gambleville. It's like some sort of fairy dust realm of economic heavenly order came about, if you let the Fed tell the story. Really, it was more like a hellish disorder. Now that these black government programs that were off the accounting books of the system, aren't getting their green hog slop of taxpayer funds needed to feed them anymore, at least in the way it was, all hell broke loose.

The multinational banks pump and dump of the public's wealth must have been leveraging this nation into debts by at least a trillion to one. For every trillion dollars of debt, only one dollar was used to pay down the principle. Sounds like the people's credit card arrangements. What a ripoff. There must have been some trillionaires walking around this empire that we have never heard about. When the times were "phat with a P"' (a slang term for "fat"), the money gangsters must have hidden a cool trillion somewhere. You know the rats that hide under the penthouse garages, far from the view of the lights. If you just look around at the damage that's being done today, it's extremely difficult for the average person to assimilate and perceive the suction of their funds that ensued.

The secret government programs were not the only handicap confronting the nation. The country could not overcome its devastating budget blows from these programs going bust, and the Nation could not afford them. They were not too big to fail, but too big to succeed. The entire scheme just was not sustainable, and now maybe neither are we. My theory is that there are no debts because there are no fundamentals in the system to which the structures of those debts can be regulated. This is one of my scream points! They have destroyed the architecture of the checks and balances on the collections system. There's nowhere to report the abuse of debt and loans by persons or corporations that have any real credibility. The bankruptcy courts are swamped with cases of grim outcomes.

There's a syndicate that operates under the dark cloak of invisibility. A compromising position that puts the country's voting system of a democracy in question of illegitimacy. Only because the secret goons don't have any oversight over them, and that alone is evidence enough to render a judgment of a lawless organization. Whenever one renegade industry starts taking instead of buying, the rule of law and freedom lacks a mandatory element of choice, which is the hallmark composition of any nation embracing the theme of rights for others.

With all the loosey-goosey easing of fiscal principals that was set into motion by various components of command, they undermined the very fabric of liberty through a process of demoting one's vote. I mean, if your vote does not count, then why do it? If the vote has been compromised, then the whole economic apparatus of a democratic government has been damaged beyond repair. I have always said, "The mo' I vote, the more I'm broke."

You would think that politicians who had so many adoring fans would want to deliver only goods of success to those honest multitudes. They would be famous instead of infamous, like they are now for the rest of their puny lives. You would think the Bush administration, which contaminated the land and was in charge for eight long havoc-wreaking years would have played their political stock differently. Once again, just a reminder. The Wall Street Journal reported that the lost decade from 1999 to

2009 was the decade of zeroes. The Nation went into a reverse of profits mode. The worst decade in the history of the stock market. No way! Yes, way!

They should have served the office for the benefit of the long-term outcomes. Be seen as a benefactor for the masses. What do the people have now? What we have always had from politicians. A lot of mouth city and no action for a better future for the many. Just another rent-a-stint at the White House hotel. They played their hands and a card laid is a card played, like they say. Not with these guys. They can take their cards back off the table and start over. The new normal is old-time cheating. They themselves have shown the results of being a short-term manipulating cast, and the masses despise them now. At least those who know can now say without a doubt that the last administration was a player in bringing on this wrath of hardship.

Now the public wants revenge on the big people. I can guarantee you that if they had it to do all over again and had another chance to lead the country with solid consultation, the administration and Wall Street would not do every crazy, selfish, lawbreaking decision they made back then. They would do everything differently, and in the best interest of the sovereign United States, right? No! We can't let stupid get in the way of facts. That's how we got off-track in the first place. Of course they would do the same things the same way again.

VII

It Still Can't Just Be Called A Crisis

How long can a crisis remain a crisis before it transforms into some other divergence? So far, since the summer of 2007, I don't know why in the world the media would only label this sharp-edged budgetary decline as being referred to mostly as the "financial crisis." I've also heard it mentioned as a nice downturn and many more generic phrases that the media club chose to classify it as. Let's just call the bleeping crisis what it is! Believe me when I say folks, "This ain't no downturn." Like I said earlier, "It's a damn crooked turn." They have used phrases like, a market slowdown, market turbulence, turmoil, or a meltdown. At some intersection of the media minds, the designation of financial crisis has to hitch its outdated wagon onto a new vernacular.

One idea is to qualify the title by examining whether the crisis has changed any of its characteristics since the credit crunch of the summer of 2007 shattered the stock exchange. During the spring of 2010, even the subtitles on the internet links about this subject on the global financial demise can make you have many a sleepless night if you know and understand what you are looking at. In the year 2007 is when the expression, "financial crisis" first went into its current duration cycle. Always using that crisis word is missing the point. It's like trying to describe the ocean by only looking through the eye of a needle. You miss the full impact of the circumstances you are presently in by limiting your vision. The same is true with catch phrases.

The politicians and Wall Street types ain't gods. We should install a new epithet for the elitists. Here, try some these other creative ideas since the media has lost the art of expanding their vocabulary. The bank lords of business should find these intriguing. Let's call the crisis: the Economic Hot Potato, or the Financial Moment of Truth, or Era of Greedy Bastards, or An Economic Explosion, or a Price Reduction Fall, or a Wage Withdrawal Syndrome, Resource Misappropriations, U.S. debt woes, a War Tax, a Boom and Bust Fund Collapse, Debt Downgrade Fatigue, a Legal Tender Tornado, a Hyper Depression, a Super Recession, Demand Destruction, an Economic Tailspin, Noah's Financial Flood, and last but not least, a Possible MF Catastrophe! I prefer the latter. What's your favorite?

Just remember that the words used by the press have a lot to do with how you perceive this throwdown of slowdowns. These fat cat banksters were also in charge at the time of the breakdown. They don't deserve to be able to call the event a disaster or any other kind of pole shift. They were asleep on the job. I was awake and on the case. Now all of these media types want to start yelling a major correction is approaching. I could have told them that back in the day. They are truly claim jumpers with no shame in their game. If they had spoken up, we may not have been in this lowdown from these clowns. Now we all may be doing the Jumping Jack Flash from the economic frying pan to the fire.

The Great Recession, as they like to call it, is the same as saying that we're in a depression-lite mode. There can be no such thing as a great recession. If it is a great recession, is that the same as a weak or mild depression? If this is only a Great Recession, who would want to see a standard depression? Not me! Yikes! If the words "financial mess" are used to give you a description of a wrecked market instead of financial doom, then you might go on and have a nice day, never thinking to investigate and see what the mess is. Is it really just a mess, or is it something much greater than a mess? I know you can see the difference between the terminology, and how it in some ways determines how your day goes. It all depends on how the news was reported. Words matter. Now we can all feel secure since I have explained this to you. Do you feel more secure? Stay well.

Overpaid for Talent

To begin with, the empire overpaid for talent. Since I am a sports fan, I'll use a sports analogy in this discussion to help clarify my point. Let's just begin with the question of why did we let matters get this far out of hand? For starters, Wall Street authorized the trainers, the towel boy, and the water girls to quit their old jobs and move on up to the eastside of town where they can profit from tons of money. Washington hired the head cheerleader himself to start on the A team.

Let's examine these statements. All during the first days of the credit crunch, you could always hear the stock market head honchos swear that the success of their business model depended on their talent pool. They would proclaim that they had the best fiscal expertise money can buy. "Nowhere else in the world can you find a better skill set. Therefore, it is absolutely imperative that we pay top salaries and bonuses to retain this talent pool. An inability to fortify our strength and maintain our staff in retrospect would be a lost opportunity to preserve our competitive edge over market share." In other words, "Pay up, foolish public, and we will dump some lumps of ding-dongs on your wealth potential. You'll pay big for the pain we've caused you and yours." they yelled.

I have to tell you that my inquiry into this matter showed me that every so-called smart head not only had an agenda that I noticed, they were more concerned with their tee times on the golf course than their company's time. We could have found this level of talent on any corner block of Wall Street. Oh, we did. It does seem like they just picked up a truckload of inexperienced stock marketeers from around the corners of Times Square, threw them inside of the money exchange, and they got to work destroying the damn thing. They were also wearing tee shirts that read, "Have you ever seen an empire die?" The workers got started creating this money monster of a nightmare right away. This fictional scenario is not true of course, but it sure seems like it could be. Look at the economic results.

There was no way that I could not notice this impending shakedown. Not enough people were—and are—talking about this event, in my opinion. I was force-fed on a CDs information overload. That is why I know about this garbage of jewels. I'm full of the same junk that you are, only you may not be aware of your plight, yet. What junk you might ask? What junk? The financial bubbles bursting, the phony people, and phony green paper. That junk! These were the same folks of assumed great talent, wisdom, and vision that led us down this contraction reaction. I mean, if these people were really talented, would we be traveling toward this atrocious predicament right now? We must look at the "Hu-man" in the mirror, to play off of Michael Jackson' song, "Man in the Mirror." Thanks, Michael, I miss you. Boy, we could sure use your being on the planet right now. There's no one to replace you, "the Magnificent Light Soul." My view is that the intelligent, bright people can and have assisted the planet up until this stage, but it's going to take the right intuitive people, like Michael, to save the planet. Not one kind of human can do it alone.

We have predominantly tried only one kind of thought processing format. That is that the intelligent brain is superior to the heart's internal brain, the avenue to the soul. As we look around at the linear mind experiment today dissolving into the abyss, there's only one other path that the world as a whole has not tried, but now may be forced to. As we are all witnessing today, now is the time for the people of the Light to assist in this undertaking with a purposeful approach. Now it's time for the right of heart to step forward into the light of day and balance the anvil of dead weight that the severely less talented have manifested upon the public neighborhood of good. I must admit, though, that not all of the poli-finance people during the era of ignorance were greedy. Some were good people of economics and fine servants of the people. They just came up against the same malnourished money monsters that we all did, and got swallowed alive.

Fire all of the lamebrain people who were right there in the rathole when the economic jailbreak happened. Some of these know-it-all types congratulated themselves daily. Put these folks out on the rocks—the so-called MVPs of finance—and get extremely competent, light, bright, wise, and resourceful gifted starters on the first team. At least you would have the best opportunity for non compromised attributes participating in the system to right the wrongs. Why not? Isn't that the goal of life, to be the best that you can be? If not, we sure spent a lot of wasted time in those mundane institutions called schools for nothing. If you ever played sports or watch sports, you know that the owners and general managers of a professional team's number one job is to acquire the best talent money can buy, so that the team can improve their chances of winning. The same is supposed to be true in all businesses and political platforms as well. Somehow that principle gets lost as the bar of honor on Wall Street and at the White House is lowered for personal gain.

Obviously these were not the kind of profit exchange teams that had a superior aptitude for business. Who were these maestros in charge of this capital rupture? The result can only equal the investment. What you put in, is what you get out. If the big bonus gangster bankers were really worth their pay, why aren't the results that we're presently experiencing financially better than they are today? Don't you think that if they were really a valuable commodity to the marketplace community at large, the outcome would be less dire than it is today? I mean, some explanation has to be given for paying these outrageous bonuses with no verification of merit. Hell, anyone of us would love to get fired and receive millions of dollars in a retirement package. Even though that's not what it's called, technically.

Tell me—anybody—have you ever heard of a person getting a lifetime retirement package after they have sunk the company's ship? Then they go on a vacation in the sunset islands for as long as it pleases them. Hey, I would take that sweetheart of a deal in a flash. Wouldn't you? Call me the next time you see a listing for a position like that. I'll relocate anywhere!

So you see, this breakdown is not because of some limited system designs. Already we have a commercial system that is sometimes adequate enough structurally for the purposes of maintaining the order of checks and balances. The financial network that's in place presently could have worked just fine if only the laws that are currently on the books had been enforced. It always astounds me that when an economic panic strikes, the first stopgap measures that governments set into motion are the ones who camouflage their ignorance of the crash facts. They would never let on that they, themselves, are not very talented either. Just average to below average. Check their grades. Or better yet, you grade the crash home-mees!

So, why do the politicos create more unnecessary laws when our existing laws have always stood the test of time? What changed? What happen to the attitude of "That's Your Tough Luck" or "You Broke It, You Fix It!"? From this country's beginning, it has been able to sustain this nation through a fiscal promise of heads you win, tails you lose. This was the business model until these misfits took over. Everybody can't win at the same time all the time. But that's where we are today. I may be wrong in my assumptions, but I don't think so.

The talent crew on the stock exchange might disagree with me, but the very nature of a financial bubble needs the assistance of a talent pool to constantly solicit clients regardless of their companies' illegal loan products. They must actualize a benefit for their shareholders at all cost. That's how the talent community continues to be gainfully employed. Nothing wrong with earning a dollar as long as it is above board, honest, and can be tracked down for tax purposes. The same duty that any citizens are obligated to do. What I'm conveying here is that not enough talent was endowed with the competency for comprehending the magnitude of World Street. It really is World Street because as Wall Street goes, so goes the world financial racket. Bye-bye!

Now that the stock market is so politically correct, just like the schools are in certain areas of the country, who knows what is what anymore? You are not allowed to fail in class—or the stock market—anymore. Everyone is basically equal in their level of intelligence. There is no difference between a mismanaged company and a well-managed company. Right? Come on, play along. No company should be allowed to fail. Right? There will be no penalties or consequences if they do hit the skids, right? That fairy dust angel is dancing in some politicians' heads again. You have to allow for failure, or else how would you ever gauge success? There would be no reason to qualify a successful company because the process would be so marginalized that you couldn't tell the difference. If there was only sunlight there, would be no rain to balance out the rest of the seasons.

It's a reason why equivalent intelligent beings seek each other's companionship out. When searching for mates, they are usually looking for commonalities. That's not the same as looking for someone who can think in another person's identical thought patterns. You need separation and differences, because if everyone thinks on the same level then you stand the risk of oversaturation, with terminal results. Here's my example of the mistakes that can be made by playing society's law of averages. Let's say one person jumps off a mountain, and because we were trained to be non-critical thinkers (kinda like we are now), then all of humanity might just jump off that mountain. Kinda like it is now! We need diversity to save the species. The lines between reality and fantasy are becoming thinner and more subjective all the time.

Also why isn't nobody stopping the public's bank accounts from getting hammered? I've always thought that if the bailout money had gone to the public instead of the banks and others, we would be witnessing a much more robust market. The talented consumer would have spent it in thrifty ways, therefore accomplishing the goal of boosting the economy. Remember, the American consumer pays for 70% or more of the U.S. economy. It was never about saving the economy. It came down to the Federal Reserve and the Washington gang saving their buddies' asses in the banks and beyond! Little do they know that it's really the little guy who's too big to fail. Without the retail investors and the consumers engaged in this process, these large corporations' talent pools will continue to vanish into thin air anyway. Soon, we may be also.

Once again I say, let the free market system weed out the bad and keep the good. Some other companies will take up the mantle where those failed companies dropped off. Always has before. Why not now? Remember the saying: Nature abhors a vacuum. I was challenged while falling behind in school, or not doing as well as I should have. It just made me work harder and smarter. I didn't need my ego stroked. I knew that I was not the smartest kid in the class. That's okay with me. It didn't destroy my motivation for success. It made me stronger. The people who were doing better in class were people I tried to emulate and improve my stats. Some students are born leaders and others are followers. It seem as though during this golden nest egg disappearance, we had the followers ahead of the truly gifted leaders. This blowback was brought to you on behalf of the disadvantaged leadership.

Generally, the stock market would spit out the weak companies and put pressure on the successful businesses for strong fundamentals. That was a long time ago. If your business defaulted because you overpaid for talent, then see ya later! These people who were working to redesign the system during these dark years should be jailed. Our funds were involuntarily included in a public game of high stakes poker (i.e., bailouts) from the government brokers. Somehow I knew that our lives would never be the same again. They sent this economy reeling! Like I said earlier, maybe us, too. Yes, we trusted and our bank accounts got busted. Somebody, please, show me the talent!

They Will Save Us

I woke up one morning doing the credit crunch in 2007 and shuddered at the thought of who was in charge of the country: the White House circus starring the untalented George W. Bush and his cronies. I knew right then that we had all signed up for the invasions and Middle Eastern conflicts whether we wanted to or not: the very same occupations that are keeping your own money from you. Let me state that both of my children, Starrlett and Rejo, served this country in these faraway desert campaigns of misguided military intentions from this leadership. These people basically traded Iraq and Afghanistan for America. A sweetheart deal for the Middle East "corporateers." A funky donkey for Americans. "They will save us and keep us safe!" were their false promises. I'm sure every American feels much more secure right now in their lives than at any other time in the nation's short 235-year history. These showcase wannabes didn't have a clue what was going on with the economy and still don't till this day. I say to myself, somebody please help me get away from these poor lost politicians and fanatics.

More people are losing their wedding rings now than ever before to pawn shops. We all have lost something very precious: our economic way of life. I can't believe or accept the fact that my generation that I'm living in has let our guard down. Now, the entire planet may be headed for not just a collapse, but maybe a hypercollision because of the mismanagement of resources. We are not the generation of the cursed. We have visions of delight for the many living creatures as a species. For all living creatures.

Some undisciplined souls can't comprehend that many things can explode and blow up our world. They do not have to come from outer space like meteors or asteroids, or like bombs from jets. Some of the largest detonations can be silent inside of mankind's weak minds. You never see the smoke or fire. The aftermath is just as deadly. This economic bomb is just such a discharge. Most people still haven't heard or felt the full impact of the reverberations yet. They will.

We as mature adults should let our collection of economic contemporaries in charge know they should be ashamed of themselves. They have endangered not only ourselves, but also spawned developments that imperiled the great pearl chance of survival, Mother Earth. They needed to check themselves before they wrecked ourselves. They are not the saviors! I vote for myself as the president of my environment. What about you?

Vengeance Versus Justice

I must speak about the U.S. court system becoming a ward of the state, seemingly powerless to correct any outstanding corruption. This is something that is at the top of the bar of lawlessness that has to be addressed. The defection of the guardians of the gates of justice is just beyond belief. The courts are supposedly the last bastion of protection for the people. Today there are no investigations or prosecutions of the giants of power. It seems as though the royal jester courts themselves need a visit from some badge-wearing skunk trappers. This urgent overhaul of injustice only points in one direction. The courts have been politicized, along with the entire deficient law scheme. The reason for the term scheme is because the moment the courts are breaking the law instead of making the law, they gave up their right to judge impartially. This is paramount to any free law-abiding civilization continuing to progress. I've seen too many popcorn westerns not to know how a lawless court can rip a town—or empire—apart by only representing the few and the powerful. They proceed into vigilantism, internal fighting, and then a dark spiral of death. Kind of like it is now.

I'm sorry to say this, but in my estimation, the U.S. court system is in rapid decay. They sold the public out for vengeance and dogma instead of justice. This is a death knell for any thriving nation. A top priority of first importance is the need to alert the court system that unless they fulfill their original intent and purpose, which is to restore a sense of honor and ethical consciousness to the system of laws, they must revoke their privilege of authority. These are the fundamental understandings that are the foundation of truth. Also, they are the grounds of any nation that wishes to remain free, sovereign, and relevant. So, make a decision, state and Federal courts. Do you continue to truly stand for justice, the rights of the people, and the nation? In that order.

Whenever the courts protect the alleged perpetrators of high crimes and treason, the courts themselves have help to establish a corruption bubble that is about to burst, and flood all the laws that have been created thousands of years ago for manmade laws. Even more powerfully arrogant by the courts is their attempt to halt the universal laws with their backdoor deals. These laws, which are eternally set in motion by a higher power, can never be altered by mankind. The question is this: Do we as a nation have laws or not? The hell with money if we don't have laws. Money without laws is a no-win situation anyway. I'd rather have laws without money, than money without laws, which is the circumstance we find ourselves in now. Wait! That's not correct. Today we have little to no laws and no money. Unlimited illegalities create instant chaos. This has to change!

Going for the Gold

We are deleveraging across world economies, thanks to both political parties. This is the colossal negative feedback loop of all time. These bureaucrats' conduct caused a shot in the face of the American Constitutional system. The non-leadership of the lost decade was despicable. Dollar signs dominated their minds. They managed to scratch out some sort of deformed strand of governing ... a lewd, twisted form of control that only their deviant minds could discern. Plans formed by financial radicals posing as government legitimates very rarely work out. These folks were eating our bank accounts alive. They got fat, happy ... and very, very rich.

Currently, these former politicians are engaged in making all the income they can by speaking at forums. It's money that should be going into a donation fund to assist the military families. The speakers of destruction want all the gold for their greedy selves. Can you even fathom that the very same people who started the greatest robbery of an empire's treasury ever had the audacity to peddle their false intentions to take the country into a terrain of bloodshed for almost a decade now and counting are going around telling the world about their success? Are things upside down or what? A sign of the times!

The Wall Street corporations were hand-in-glove with these operations. They profited from the forced offensive tactics as well. Most of the instigators of the U.S. occupations are out of office at this present day. They are traversing America and the world as though the country is in peacetime. I guess even they are tired of thinking and living through the invasions they started. Did they finally figure out that these efforts are really draining on the American people's consciousness and finances? A nation of this size still has got to have some big stooges that still need to be investigated, or go to jail if found guilty. All these actors can't be innocent.

Big Mouths

The great question of our present times is, who is responsible for this cashless conundrum? Well, we may not be certain about all of the folks that brought this about, but we can safely say who did not cause this dollar damage. Let's start with the poor people of any nationality: the Blacks, the Mexicans, the Indians, and many other financially concerned citizens that had no hands on the Wall Street crystal ball. No way could they have caused this fiscal slam-bam. We all came up against what I call, "The big, bad wolf syndrome"—American leaders who transformed this country's image and reputation into a cloud of braggadocio.

Anytime that they did not agree with your stance, they would claim to huff and puff and blow your house down. Remember Cindy Sheehan? They tried to blow her away, but she never surrendered. This government is one loop of despair that has to get corrected somehow. The politicians, military leaders, and lobbyists have blown a gaping black hole into the character of this once proud, renowned and great superpower. How does it get fixed? Here are a few possible suggestions that I considered during 2007 to 2008.

First in relation to the stock market, there were many days that when if any of these people from the Bush administration, including Bush himself, showed their face on the TV screen, the market would take a nosedive at light speed. Whenever they would open their big mouths, look out below in the stock market. The media outlets that supported this administration for all those dark years became afraid to give them any airtime toward the end of their terms, like it is nowadays. No airtime for these people who need to be on air explaining what happened. You might ask yourself why the market would tank if the economy was doing so well in 2007-08.

Simply put, I can sum it up in one word. Trust. The minute, I mean, the second these Jaspers started flapping their lips from Paulson to the Fed chair, Ben Bernanke, the investors would shrill in terror. The market would disintegrate. Then the parasitic media would send out the recovery team and snow job the public, telling them why the market did so badly. You can fill in the blank. They would proclaim, "The reason that the stocks really took a beating has nothing to do with politics. It's only whatever we said is happening and nothing else." Always protecting and never revealing that the airheads in Washington were connected to the failure. I knew the retail investors wanted new leadership, and there was none to be found.

The money market independent researchers on the Internet were much more ahead of this story than the desperadoes in the White House and Wall Street. We knew that you could not even compare what is happening currently to the Great Depression. This could end up being many times worse. In 2008, I called the event "The Greater Depression." I think I'll change that title to "The Extreme Deleveraging." We could be in the last inning of the game of life. Maybe years, maybe months or weeks, is all the time we have left to make our peace in the world.

So, what's the remedy? Many investors back in the day, long ago (you know, 2007-08) wanted someone to be held accountable for the erosion of the sovereignty of the free market. If you've been really following this epic disgrace, you know who the people are who need to possibly be arrested in the opinionated free-marketeers' eyes, or at least questioned. Let's face it, friends, these folks have killed the golden goose and there have been no ramifications for their dereliction of duty. Well, the investors thought differently, and you can see their effects. Because of the lack of regulatory inactions in the institutions, the free marketeers bolted.

Now the key players are running around free as you or me. Only we have never taken an oath to the citizenry to uphold and protect the Constitution, which makes the free market enterprise possible. Just look at where the market is currently. I knew that by holding the "deciders" and the Street money executives to their sworn obligations, perhaps the market could have survived. That is not what has evolved. These servants are hiding behind the townspeople. I guess there is no honor among thieves. If they are the alleged characters of destruction and it is proven in a court of law, then let the citizens prevail with all of the might of integrity on their side. That day justice will shine bright on America again. This has been screamed by many for years. It's not news. Some of you are just late to the dance. As Bruce Willis said in "Die Hard," "Welcome to the party, pal!"

The Press Going Out of Business

The media totally abandoned the nation years ago, and it's still happening. All the while this shipwreck was going down, the mainstream press, who were supposed to be the first and last defenders of the people from the sharks on Wall Street and in Washington, were MIA: missing in action in many cases. In the end, the journalism beast became confused about where this slithering snakebit economy was headed. I could have answered that befuddling question for them. I knew by their actions that they did not want to ask the hard questions and wrack their brain.

We as a species needed copiousness amounts of leadership and guidance from Wall Street and the White House, but there was none to be found. When I first started to devote my time to this phenomenon in 2006, there were mostly only positive analyses and articles on the economy.

At that time, everyone was so sure that the real estate industry would never, ever blow up. So the flowery, passionate media, determined to be right, drank the Bush administration's poison Kool-Aid, hook, line and drinker … and we all sank. We are still sinking. Only the difference now is that the tempo has increased a millionfold. Can't you feel it? It's hard to miss.

Now the members of the press can feel it, too, but they are on the slow show. How could so many be so asleep at the wheel? They were not asleep. They were zombified from orders high up in the chain of command. That's right. I'm saying that the media is basically connected to the same multinational corporations that created the war invasions. That's old news. Right? I don't know how anybody could not be confused after this sham. The only way that I was able to make the right calls on the market was to not listen to these people because I knew they were lost. When I took my retirement funds completely out of the market in 2008, I had to have a clear vision to make that call. I made a run on my bank during this same time. The bank supervisor thought I was premature on getting some of my dollars changed to small bills. These were fire and brimstone times. Extremely difficult and challenging. That's what it was like for me back in the days.

Major life decisions were going down in my family while most were thinking about where they were going on their next vacations. The cloak of economic collusion was in a sprint toward the finish line of stock market obliteration. If I had been listening to the commentators, I would have gotten burned and lost many of my financial assets like most everybody else did in 2008. At least I got to spend it! The government and the Street didn't! A moral victory, at least. Hey, there's a capital collection plate with your name on it that's getting passed around in Congress. They're seeking tax contributions and your treasures without your permission every second of the day now. Consumer beware!

This was no time for political gamesmanship. This was survival of the financial fittest. As a matter of fact, in the spring of 2009 during a visit to my accountant, he surprisingly gave me unexpected praise for being the only one of his clients to steer clear of Wall Street in 2008. The rest of his clients lost their shirts. I wonder how much money the newsmasters lost in their retirement accounts in the market during these times. That would be a nice stat to know. Probably tons! These were the same people most were listening to at that time. Suckers! You lost most of your funds believing in your fairly godfathers. There was no way the public could know. I felt and still feel so much sorrow for them. How could the public know with these show-and-tell minstrels running interference for the machine? The mass stream media never slam-bashed the black magic show offered by these back-stabbing, profit-taking warlocks. They needed to stop the madness of the "Fed-o-nomics" enslaving the free markets. They just didn't know, I guess. Neither did you! That why it is important where you get your information from. It could mean life or death these days.

The force of the fictional talking heads actually had no doubt that they were right! Anyone who had an opposing view to theirs was verbally accosted ... possibly blacklisted and considered to be insane. Let's just name a few of the top pro-choice war hawks who did not have a clue about the economic troubles that lay ahead. We can begin with the mouth almighty Rush Limbaugh. This guy swayed this country with his all-surefire declarations that were disgustingly inaccurate. Here are a few others that graduated from the Rush school of distrustful journalism: Sean Hannity, Larry Kudlow, Tucker Carlson, David Shuster, and too many more to name at this point. Let's just keep this simple, folks. These commentators caused more terror in the hearts of America and the world than any bombs that were dropped. Words are things that can hurt and confuse the citizens.

Now that the entire world can see that they were abhorrently wrong about the Middle East and multiple situations, not even one of them has admitted guilt to getting the calls wrong. Not one! Now, these are some fine upstanding announcers that you can store your trust in. Not! As a matter of fact, instead of doing the honorable deed, which would be to claim their shame and resign from their positions of power, they are ramping up the disinformation to the hundredth power. I wonder when was the last time these people had a visit to the shrink? We all need a visit after they ran their delirious campaign of dread and pain upon the nation. These people are the really dangerous ones. The super sad state of affairs that's causing the decomposition of the U.S. sovereignty is not in some faraway land, but sitting right behind a microphone in a studio somewhere in the promised land.

Now here's the tear-dropper. After a decade or so of missing the calls, many herds of humans are still listening to these merrymakers. What's it going to take for the good people to wake up? If the mouthpiece for the multinational corporations don't step down from their positions of authority, how will America ever clear it's disastrous future omens that these incompetent control media collaborated to create? It easy to talk your way into a Great Depression without proper functional oversight. It's impossible to stop the death spiral once it's set in motion.

I saw grand economic stories of the day, and the networks purposely ignored them, but the investors didn't. I did learn a little bit from drowning in this fiscal cesspool. It's hard for the media to fool the investors and traders as a whole. These people watch their pennies. Maybe that's what's wrong with the Washington standard of finance. The politicians feel as though they have no skin in the game. It's the taxpayers' loot anyway. It really works in a totally opposite process that's difficult for the higher-downs to comprehend. They took an oath to protect the taxpayers' interest. Doesn't that mean anything to them? They have their soul's skin in the game. It's called Karma. What goes around comes around. That's even more of a burden to the beast than the money. Wow! Such young incarnate souls. Besides without the stock exchange working properly, there can be no government that can provide the citizens with the services that are necessary to maintain stability and peace. It's mandatory to avoid unwarranted interruptions. Unintended consequences can lead to a small inconvenience for the government by the masses.

Like, for example, rioting in the streets of the nation-state! Just a thought of one such mishap that could arrive as a result of the inactivity. Non-reacting teams of so-called leadership can do bad all by themselves.

No one in the darling mainstream media of the U.S. had the fortitude to challenge the all-powerful racketeers. The men and women all just hunkered down instead of doubting authority. That should be the media's primary duty: to truthfully inform the sheeple. Other than that, what good are they? What's their purpose besides covering up for the companies of commerce? So as we float into the abyss of counteractive lifestyles, I suspect that in the near future there will be less media. The major media outlets are falling like the "religitic" flunkies that they are. Deservedly so!

When the press became a dogma many decades ago, their usefulness had already expired. If they only had championed for the good and the right of the citizens. Chances are they would still have a journalism career to support their lifestyle. I will never understand why would a person give up their business and life-earning potential for a temporary political ploy that's here today and gone tomorrow. No person or organization is worth sacrificing my livelihood.

Maybe old Cheney can throw the innocent laid-off network employees who had nothing to do with the administering of this dollar debacle, a bone from his profitable engagements. The CEOs and Bush can start a support group for the media funds and cover all the good ole boys and girls of the press who sugar-coated the fictional landscape of finance on their behalf. "Being rich is the only way to live." This mantra misled the masses. Still, to this day, the politicians and banker types are being shielded. I'm impressed by the press's devotion till the end toward these untrustworthy servants of the people. The media generally protected these folks, and now they are going out of business because, in some cases, the protector did not get a fair deal.

The press should have slammed the last presidential administration for disobedience and a disregard for upholding the ethical honor to the highest executive office in the world. The press is not going to get a second chance to get it right. It's lights out now. Thanks to the folks you protected with your power of the printed and spoken word, you have been awarded a nice care package. You are on your way out the door. The loss of your job is your gift from corporate. Don't forget to hang the "Going Out of Business" sign that's on your desk on the door on your way out.

Also the cloned correspondents on TV that pretend to report the latest news are men and women on a mission, should they decide to accept it. Reporters, too, must write within the media companies' guidelines … or they don't write at all. So, getting factual information is a perplexing problem. You just have to practice at it like any other skill you desire to develop. Understanding these all-encompassing, intricate, and deceptive blueprints of Wall Street rewiring the infrastructure of global finance is the reason I wanted to make my own discovery about the decimated wealth of the middle-class Americans. Lately, another mega-loop is developing. First there were the home loan defaults and foreclosures, commonly known as the subprime slime. The next shoe that is bombing the market is commercial real estate. Now I'm seeing countries starting to default on their debt. Could the overleveraged U.S. be far behind in the pipeline? I'm smelling the odor of another subprime dying? Maybe not ... I hope not.

The TV guys did have some worthy guesses on the air that told the story of this money mirage straight as they saw it. They were validating that I knew what I was talking about, because they said the same things I was thinking about. Most of the TV hosts didn't know the lowdown. Some of their guests did. In the first half of 2007, this story was burning up hot on the Internet. Well, the main media outlets are never gung ho for a slam on a Wall Street story. Besides, a lot of the times, Wall Street provided their gravy train or, should I say, paychecks. Back then, they would try to do some hard reporting sometimes. Nowadays, the investigating is all so soft. The cotton ball is the only thing softer than this monetary reporting of today.

I never understood why anyone in the Internet age would allow some stranger in a TV station or radio station to be their news programmer. You should be your own news programmer and search just a little deeper into subjects of critical relevance. I don't mean to inconvenience anyone, but if there was ever a time to take news seriously about the climatic changes, the economy, the scientific or military fate, in that order, now is it. This is the time for each and every one of us to become a personal agent for change.

I have always felt that the shadow government has always held mankind back from the true science of our heredity, beings whose manifest purpose is to have an inner eclipse where you go from darkness into conscious lightness. Well, the way things are going, at least I'll have the satisfaction of knowing that their selfish goals will be difficult to achieve. Also with less black op money in the bank, the very thing that the press was supposed to disclose is the very thing that ate them alive. The truth!

The whole global financial crack-a-jack misinformation network of communications is as lost today as a deer standing in New York's Times Square during the lunchtime rush hour. Now these wannabe like the Joneses scrap writers and their chief of speaks are lost in the womb of doom. They're trying to swim their way out of the gunk and murkiness, seeking to recover the Wall Street's former high reputation.

Like a heavyweight fighter who won the championship belt by default, the paper pushers could not take a hit in the gut for honor ... even if their lives depended on it. Oh, their lives do depend on it. For the life of me, I can't grasp why the publication agencies would listen to these flunkey money grabbers who were all mouth and gut wind. Easy answer. They got paid, baby! This must change yesterday! Guess what? It already has changed. Only they just don't know it yet, but they will. Soon, everyone will.

Actors, Athletes, and Musicians Revolt

The next revolutionary suggestion I have envisioned to expedite a transition of enlightenment is for sports stars, musicians, actors, and actresses to make it an imperative action that before each game or concert, sometime during the event, they are obligated to speak on current issues of the day that are relevant to their fans and the world. If not, why would they have twenty sports stations on basic cable TV and only one financial station, and it's not on 24 hours a day. The athlete must point out abuses of the government on their nation. If they don't do this, they could lose their livelihood, kind of like the direction it is heading toward today. Even the celebrities and entertainers are losing paydays. Their money is going up in smoke and not one yet have I seen screaming. They are getting scammed and slammed by the rip'em and drip'em dry money networks of corruption also. Their salaries are shrinking at a fast rate.

You see, the sports stars will be losing money left and right, and still, no one is speaking up. I think it's partly because they don't know yet what hit them. When they figure out what happened to them and theirs, there will be Hades to pay! Not! As long as they are still making lots of money and the gravy train is still running they will sit on their cabooses and ride the tracks to wherever they may lead. But if that train ever breaks down or, worse yet, closes down the train station altogether, that is when you will hear from them in numerous emotional, rebellious ways.

At least they could have shined a light on the problems on the stock market and could have pointed out the counterfeiters and stopped the swindle before it got going good, maybe. This ain't the old days, where you can only be a pro ballplayer or a musician or entertainer. The "just live for your art" days are over. You and everybody else are under attack from an enemy from within. This is exactly the reason I'm writing this book: to empower the citizens to trust their own intuition. It's as good as anybody else's. I guess when enough people don't have enough to survive on, the pace will be picking up for wanting some sort of accountability for this madness.

Fantasy Theory

Let's imagine there were no invasions and occupations that were cooked up in the neocons' boiler rooms that bamboozled most of the body politic, the media and the lion's share of the public. Snow jobs were crammed down the loyal subjects' throats at a rapid pace and with depth. Let's say loyalty actually was upheld and cherished by the honorable folks in power. Life would be nice without the massive propagandized scam campaigns for the rich. Some people even imagined their money staying in this country, building things for the townsfolk that pay for them, not paying for destroying things in faraway lands for the sake of so-called fake freedom ego trips. I know this sounds so utopian, but now all these other countries are now speaking about preserving their economies as being a top priority. Take care of number one first. America has started so many fires that I truly hope that they can be put out by the time the economy demands a drastic pullback on spending for this once great superpower.

The governing body would be heroes if the nation stood up for what's right. Everywhere the administration went, there would be genuine adoration for them. Sounds like pre-election jungle hoopla running at a fever pitch. Think about pre-election promises. Now, fantasize that your body politic safeguarded and activated those guarantees that mistakenly slid out of their lips. This is the case for every officer of the future when they first begin campaigning for office. They have a chance to go straight and maintain their bonds of trust, but in countless cases the bonds are broken. Why is it that so many who took the oath defecated on the privilege? Maybe because the system itself is damaged.

You would think that with so many opportunities to succeed with the citizens' support, something grand and wonderful would materialize out of it for the nation and the world at large. At least once! If this were the case as it should be, jobs would be in abundance in this country, and not in the Middle East. I guess just fanciful dreaming doesn't create the reality of employment … or does it? Many infuriated citizens cannot survive the lost decade of zeroes presented to them by the fast-wheeling-and-dealing last administration. There are not many heroes in politics today, but there are millions of heroes outside of politics: the general public. The average citizen. You. What they have asked of the civilians is a tremendous price to pay. The economic pain and suffering is just too great of a load. We can help stop ourselves from being known as the last generation of the money Mohicans. Well, at least we can all dream that the future is brighter. Can't we?

VIII

Sleeping Giants Have Awakened

Practically everyone is missing the best part of the eight-year results from the Bush administration. I mean these global financial markets are rocking and rolling. This was a multi-level corporate heist. Wall Street had no idea that they would awaken giants that should not be disturbed. They were told by our ancestors during the last great depression that they were not allowed to step foot into this valley of the forbidden financial fruit trees again. Does this sound like a story you have heard of before? "Don't eat the forbidden fruit! Don't let investment banks merge with commercial banks. Yet, somehow the financial moguls did not read the clear signs saying 'wrong way, go back!'

There were many big wigs on Wall Street that were obliviously brain dead to the facts. Over-confident that they could never be wrong, they marched on toward the land of no return. Oh, there were many opponents screaming at the top of their lungs, "Stop! You must never approach this fiscal territory! That is where the monsters of economic downfall reside! Don't wake them!" Wall Street was told again and again! Not enough political and economic willpower around to investigate the warning seriously. Little to no oversight on Wall Street and the White House has caused these crippling currency monstrosities hampering the world's awakening.

By this time the negative feedback loops are lined up like the stars in the night sky. Only it's not totally decided yet if these alignments are twinkling in our favor. Do the stocks of the stars have humanity's interest at heart? Actually, there is no heart involved in any of these scams. From the stock market, which is basically the banking giants, to the main street consumers, the contract assassination is in full motion. What I'm writing about is the heinous drumming sounds echoing and rumbling throughout the empirical stomping grounds, Wall Street, and Washington. There will be economic giant footsteps smashing down all around us soon. They just couldn't resist the urge to get filthy rich. Happens every time when you let politics override law. Now everything in the stock market feels herky-jerky.

This Wall Street drama reminds me of the movie "2001: A Space Odyssey," written by the great Arthur C. Clarke and developed by the brilliant director, Stanley Kubrick. Remember HAL, the computer with all of its technological promise that was supposed to save the mission? Sounds like the assurances we got from the financial wizards on Wall Street and the politicians. Then there was the danger that comes alone with the risk of unmeasured oversight of controlling the Wall Street machine. No one could stop it from turning back on us and eating us alive. Sadly, this is a common theme of then and now.

Market Down, Man Down

Some of the companies I wrote about earlier could lead to the greatest setbacks we currently face as a country. Since reevaluating my thoughts, I discovered that one of the most undesirable loops that the world must take note of is here now. It is causing all of the difficulties we are challenged with today. Wall Street is shaking like a hyperquake. Unemployment today is not just about the loss of a career because of some type of discrimination about age or race. It has now devolved into human discrimination touching everyone's lives.

I remember there was a time in this country it was assumed that you could find employment somewhere. From teenagers to older adults, you could find some trade that suited you for at least a little while to help you make it through a tough spot. That allowed job seekers a comfort zone. The youngsters don't know how good we had it back then and they never will. Of course, the up and coming budding adults do not want to hear about the way it was. Looking around at the current financial conditions, I can't say that I blame them. They want job results now. Why can't they get a job? Why are the young college students and graduates finding it almost impossible to land employment? Why must they live at home with their parents at this stage in their lives? I will make an attempt to give an overview of why this is so.

Perhaps because something has gone really wrong. We all fell through the occupational cracks which have widened to record widths. Who knew that we as a nation could fall down so far? It's easy when we had no leadership, who was supposed to be minding the store! The fall can only be equivalent to the rise. Let's just say for the sake of conversation that you took your boat out in fifty feet of water. Now you are in control and all is calm. But suppose that you get word on your radio that a thousand-foot tsunami was advancing your way very rapidly. With no time to get away, you choose to ride the wave with all of your might. Now you are located directly on top of that monster wave looking down. What do you think you would see, being on top of that thousand-footer?

I can tell you the answer to that. A major crash of water and debris coming down that will level the place soon. You are at peak time and horrified about what you know is coming next. The "Mother of all Wipeouts!" That's kind of where we are financially. It's all dropping down on our heads right now. I think. You can never be absolutely sure about these massive matters. I just take my best shot, hold on, and hope for the best.

Now everyone is passing the buck. Blaming the other guy for falling down on the job. Of course no one on the Street saw this wreck coming, either. There are so many dominoes still waiting to fall. There will be no mass employment any time soon. To stop this falldown would be the same as taking a pig out of a python. I'm reversing the old saying. Maybe to stop this downsizing of the money this time around, they'd have to extract an elephant out of a python. If the gospel truth be told, there are mind-boggling reductions still ahead for the multitudes' finances.

One of the most confusing confrontations ever known to mankind is the fact that there are so many scenarios that are too big to fail. Which one do I follow today? If certain corporations did take a nosedive, they would harm the planet's balance of financial fundamentals for eons to come. For instance, there are the military's wars on multiple fronts and wherever else they are engaged in that we don't know about. One day they, too, will run short of funds. Look out below when that happens. Then, there's the world banking system which will have to answer for the business emergencies they have created. The political systems of many countries would have to answer where they were when economic crimes were being committed on their watch.

I saw the Federal Reserve use up all of its wad—printing money faster that you can shake a stick at. Where do we go from here? Then there's the dysfunctional regulators such as the Congress, the Senate, the SEC the CBO, the IRS, and others who missed the breakup of the banking system. There's also the missing-in-action providers of justice who should have cut these suspect bookie operations off at the path. The nation's law enforcement agencies. The Department of Justice, the FBI, CIA, FDIC, Homeland Security, and a host of other hustlers that the citizens are bankrolling, were all snoozing when this thing blew up on their watch.

Are you surprised? I'm not. Which one of these outfits is supposed to investigate this kind of commercial crime scene anyway? Someone should have looked into this decades ago, long before it went this far and got out of hand. Every last one of these mismanaged companies is expendable, in my opinion. We can do bad all by ourselves. Look around at how rough it is on the common folks and the well-to-do crowd as well. This event plays no favors. We don't need these king and queen of setbacks ruining the success that we could have without them. These hazardous operations are some of the reasons for the dark drumbeats of depression, economically and mentally, that we are facing today.

Finally, there are two facts about the Great Depression that we should consider as a nation. One is that the Great Depression in this country was mostly experienced by whites on one level and other races on another level. Remember there were many nationalities that did not have voting rights back then. Now, that has all changed. We all will be competing for the same goods and supplies now, legally and illegally! Another fact is that in the Great Depression, the banking and government systems pulled back on spending and set off the collapse in motion. Currently we are in a depression, in this author's opinion, and the U.S. politicians have not begun to reverse their policies on wild spending sprees.

Just about all of the statesmen and stateswomen have played a hand in determining our route of doubt. They supplied the honey for the Wall Street grizzly. It's sad to have to write this but that infamous honey is: no oversight under any circumstances of the global markets and government spending in recent years. Just what the bear needed coming out of hibernation. The bureau's mechanisms of enforcement could not recognize this and adjust fast enough for the quickening of the oncoming "choke and stroke" of the stock exchange. These fools and the rest of the security agencies should have been keeping their eyes on what Wall Street was up to, instead of Main Street. Now they are all in trouble!

They will be downsizing soon or going out of business. The market fell straight on its back and the operational management teams of these large public procurement programs for funds could not assist in the resuscitation. Just think how much better off the nation and the global financial structural system would be if some of these agencies had been awake enough to start screaming their heads off about this destruction by deficits that we were facing. I guess they were caught totally off guard. "Surprise, surprise!" ... Gomer. Let's hope that because of their failure to enforce protocols in agency procedures, the human race won't go into hibernation. Permanently!

The Non-Bankruptcy Bankruptcy

The master of all screwed-up feedbacks is the nonbankruptcy bankruptcies. Let me decode that statement for you. Now, all the rage of the bankruptcy courts is to let the mega-corporations file for default and tell them that not all of the company will be put into reorganization. The courts will let the profitable parts of the company continue to operate as close as it can to a normal business model. The so-called parent will take the hit in court. The phrase often used to describe this racket is good bank, bad bank. It's equivalent to saying that if you go into bankruptcy, you can keep your good credit standing on certain assets such as your bank account and file for default on your bad debt. That way, you can still operate so that you won't lose access to your money, even though in bankruptcy proceeding, you probably shouldn't have a bank account. In other words, they are letting the conglomerates break more rules than you or I could ever conceive in a million years and get away with it.

They are basically avoiding a total collapse of the franchise by letting them cook the books and force them to require certain write-offs that would leave the companies standing. It also reinforces the model of zombieism, where a firm just exists on very shaky financial footing. They are in bankruptcy but they not in bankruptcy. They are the corporate undead. That's after the judge said that this would be a fast-track bankruptcy. That's where we are. If you were filing for bankruptcy, wouldn't you like to have one of those fast-track bankruptcies? That's where you can get rid of your bad debt by simply discarding it from the record books, with the judge's permission, of course. You get to use your good debt for rebuilding a new credit file. Sweet! Where can I buy one of those? You can't. They are only for the chosen few and we ain't one of them! "So take a hike, you debt slave." Only the multinational corporations are eligible for the fast-track bankruptcies. "So squirm, the rest of you mice tax suckers" … or maybe we are the 'suckees.' Either way it sucks.

Everyone is in the same boat of uncertainty now. It didn't help matters at all that back in 2005, "President Bust" signed into law a new bankruptcy change of rules stating basically, that if Joe or Jane Public goes into default, they can never get out of that debt and it must be repaid at the full cost. Before this law went into effect, you could eventually be relieved of your debt, refresh your credit slate clean, and start over after a period of seven years or so, depending on the kind of BK. Now, that option is not available to you, thanks to the lobbyists for the credit card companies, the U.S. Congress, and the lost-in-space administration of old George W. Bush himself. Remember, this is the same administration that wanted to invest the Medicare and part of your pension funds into Wall Street back in the day. It's a good thing cooler heads prevailed and stopped this monster disaster plot. We would be in much more dire conditions than today if this hare-brained scheme had developed.

I Became a Bummer Loop

Most of my friends call me RJ or Rejo. They know that I'm not a complainer. But I became a disheartened feedback loop while checking in on the cash crash. Just ask my wife. She is so tired of me proclaiming this and that about the banking fiasco. I can dig it, too. I'm sick of hearing myself rant on about this forced financial failure rite of passage. How she puts up with me, I'll never know. The confusion of having me around, bringing up the subject of the clowns downtown at Wall Street is an old and dusty jewel of a conversation in our residence. Frankly, at this time in the game, so many years later, I'm disgusted when hearing about this same old tired story myself. I know how my wife of over 20 years must feel, listening to me jabbering on about this system's demise. This ain't the happiest topic to talk about. In 2008, we were going back and forth about our retirement plans for the future. It was a heated time in our household. We jumped ship back then and got out!

Still, she would ask me from time to time, what's going on in the market? Sometimes I would tell her and sometimes I would not because I was not in the mood to elaborate on the subject. It's for sure wearing on our relationship, which is only normal. I try to keep us balanced. Soon all couples will be having these dialogues in their homes. We are just some of the first to deliberate these matters of contention because of my interest in the subject. I'm just someone addressing the issue of the day: a quickly deteriorating world of commerce. I'm in between the people and the numbskulls who jammed up the market system. It's a lonely existence for my intellectual mind to live.

These mortal morons of the greenback brigade force-feed us clown cakes that were loaded with the illusions of treasures aplenty. Any time a dime-a-dozen hustler approaches you, turn around and go the other way. Didn't your mother give you the lowdown on this golden rule? The problem is the hustler has the ID code to your bank account with the bank's permission. How do you top that? "Just take two bailout pills and call me in the morning when you arrive at the breadline for breakfast."

Some of my greatest pain originates from not being able to tell folks the update on the latest word. I tell people before I give them some grim news that it's better to break their heart than to let them get destroyed. That doesn't make it any easier. I always ask first, are you sure you want hear this bunch of crap that will sting and zap you? Most people don't, including me. I myself can't tolerate me sometimes, so I can imagine what others might think of me. Many times I just keep my big trap shut and don't say a word. This is sad for me to do, to not let innocent Earthlings know what the crooks are cooking up against them. Sometimes when I'm alone I whimper in my beer. No one knows this. I guess now they will, but what's an economic crash vet to do? I bit off much more than I can chew.

Early on in this process I have to admit, that it was like a thrill-seeking ride. My adrenaline would get to flowing about the events that were going down. I could get some kind of a rush from it. I would feel like I had this big daddy rich story under control. Every extreme rush has a precarious enemy. Reality. I was overwhelmed at the magnitude and perplexities of the market dilemmas. I had to cope with the mind-numbing thought that this predicament might not turn around, maybe not even in my lifetime. Whoa!

Get my point. Here I am living in this hellhole of voluminous statistical nonproficiency staring at me head on. Some days it felt like my comprehension of the market was squared to the 10th power. I had a clear vision of this story. Then other times I was just flat-out lost in the numbers. It all took a toll on me after a few years of being in the money pits of deception. I have not been the same since. If the public just could have been free of this economic con job, we wouldn't have to be feeling the pinch-an-inch techniques eating a hole in our bank notes right now.

How could I not scream at the top of my lungs with the knowledge I had stumbled upon? What good is this information if I don't share it? I asked myself this question daily. Then an even more challenging apprehension entered my mind. What if my purpose in life is to inform others of these facts? Was I born to be some kind of messenger? Why would a guy with just a basic educational background leap out to familiarize himself about the acute condition of the world of commerce? I still have no answer for that question. Sometimes I wish I was as uninformed as most folks. At least it would make the day go by easier.

The downside to that stance, though, is that you could get bushwhacked by an unexpected event. Sometimes, I dislike who I have become and other times I'm glad I have the knowledge. I pick my poison daily. You would never know it because I don't wear it on my sleeves, but sometimes the misery of knowing is too much to bear. No therapist would have a clear understanding of what I'm talking about. I am at least three years ahead of the average person. The funny thing is that even though I might be farther alone in my knowing, we are going to all ride the same train to the station of shambles, at the same time, if this train doesn't get turned around.

Personally speaking, I'm not a bummer kind of a guy. I'm a "positoid," a word I created to describe a person that's like walking sunshine in motion, generally fun to be around. I'm someone who can make everyone I'm around feel better. Hey, I've been playing music for kids for over twenty years. I'm the ultimate Mr. Happy. This subject is just a bummer subject, but I'm trying to find the hope. What's a bummer is that the wholesale scheme of profit for the few and not for the many caused was by stupidity and avarice. This has not only depleted the nation's treasuries, but the very soul of the people's belief in a system of commerce. The citizens just don't know it yet. I had to learn that the hard way through trial and error. I'm just sick of the whole crap. I just wanna have fun.

Birdland

I've have had the privilege of feeding and hanging out with wild turkeys and deer for many years now, believe it or not. I've been passing the word how we humans have screwed up their and our environmental paradise. I said to them that something big is coming down soon. I was telling them about how the universal law of cause and effect works, and how most humans don't obey these laws enough. Basically, it's very simple to explain for most people and animals to understand … not so easy for world leaders to interpret. It goes like this: If you do this, that will happen. If you do that, this will happen. In other words, for every action you make, there's an equal and opposite reaction that's also activated into motion in the universe. There's no free lunch. Pay for your crimes now or pay later. There's no escaping. So when you see the world conditions that we are now experiencing, just know that this is no coincidence or mistake. Someone, or many people, committed certain acts that created the pain that's engulfing the modern species of today. We are just witnessing the results of that law. That is something only the wise and the animal lovers will understand. Just a little side note.

Many species of animals are relocating now all over the planet. The pattern of the animals at my house has changed drastically. Many insect and animal die offs are currently in progress all over the planet. For the people who are not in tune to the animals, they should start to notice what is going on around them. As far as the wild animals and domestic creatures are concerned, they too are programmed to migrate to environments that improve their chances of survival. Fisherman are surely seeing a difference in the waters. Probably the hunters that hunt the wild game animals are seeing a difference in a reduction of population available to hunt. Where are all the animals migrating to? I don't have the answer to that, but it does concern me. It is widely known from the ancient times that as the animals go, so do we. We are the weak link in the food chain of survival. Humans would be some of the first to go if things get out of hand like they seemingly are today. Treat the animals with respect, for who knows how much longer they will be around. That also goes for the human beast.

Funny Johnny-Come-Lately's

All these funny Johnny-Come-Lately's makes me so exasperated that I have nothing but disregard for these misfits. I kept saying to myself all through 2007 when the bunk hit the jet stream that the Congress and the Senate were in sleep mode. I said one day these war dregs of lostness will come running out of the barn when the horses have already escaped with the money in the saddlebags. Once again, the breakdown and the no-shows of these repeat slow-to-go reactor types are the very patterns of impediment that is pushing the sand of the economic dust storm against our path of success. How dare they put up a front like they know who, what, when, and where the loot is hidden and who has it? I saw the loot being robbed. I have a better insight on who does not have the loot. You and me!

We have been lifted of our life savings and our near future. The financial game has failed the people miserably, and the people failed to hold the cheaters to a level of examination and demonstration before truth is accepted. How could we know with so many military distractions? That is really totally unfair for a tax system of the public funds to ask the citizens to try and get a job in this tough economy. In most cases, just raising a family is a grind all by itself. They want us to also do the politician's job for them, which is to regulate the nation's laws to the best of their ability. That's just asking too much of us. Don't we get it yet? The present political and financial landscapes that have been created by these people are the best that they can do! Losers!

If the people had woken up in time to see the arrogance of the bonuses Wall Street was paying its employees, maybe a red flag could have been raised. That's the oath takers job, isn't it? This is not even mentioning the bankers' salaries. These are just the bonuses of the perceived wealth. Here's my limited interpretation of the bonus program. Many employed on the stock exchange received most of their pay not through weekly paychecks, but with an end-of-the-year balloon bonus bonanza. So this is another connection to the grapevine of slime. The moonshine fandango at the year's end is the reason for the season for these fancy shoes and fancy suits, lords of the liar loans. They make and rake in the loot during this camouflaged opportunity to shine. The more phony paper they can disassemble onto the market throughout the annual, the more they stand a chance of securing for themselves a personal fortune of profits at year's end. Which explains one of the engines of the runaway train of noneconomic discipline.

Have they made each of us earthlings irrelevant to the planet by their stash-the-cash schemes? I know that's not the case. We are the force that can at least wake up to the possibility of making this subject more discussed in everyday circles. That would elevate humanity and begin the process of healing from all this stealing.

Faith-based Economics

It seems as though some kind of fanatical Christian renegade cult invaded the true followers of Christianity. I can't totally get the entire picture, but the politics smells fishy inside of the nation's main religions. What are the standards of the congregation when it comes to jailing deviants whose affiliation with the denomination are only for political abuse and personal gain? I believe that we also had a theology bubble burst at the same time that the housing bubble was bursting. BushCo was slinging their God phrases out of their mouths like they were some kind of "holy saint" during this time. Little did the loyal communion know that they had been infiltrated from within by these allegedly distrustful servants of the Lord. Religion is a great place to hide. There's no one guarding the hopeful house.

This has great implications. Most faithful just assume that the leadership of the church is honest. But what if they do not have the best interests of the flock at heart? What happens if none of the leaders that you depend on were trustworthy? Are there consequences for their actions? If there are, then the church would be doing a better job at policing their premises than the White House, or Wall Street for that matter. These dogma schemes are complicated to figure out. What's really going on with these organizations? Man, am I glad that my spiritual path can be achieved alone. We'll just have to see where this all ends up.

All I know is that in my lifetime, I don't think I have ever seen an honest president that did not break the nation's laws. Many are so dogmatic that they are perhaps more bounded by the Bible before the Constitution. Who knows anymore? Anyone with this agenda makes my blood run cold. Only because they are primarily so concerned with doing the church's work and forget about the people's business. I don't care about your religious persuasion—just don't let it interfere with the nation's Constitutional duties. Looks like it's too late for that! In other words, refrain from instilling your faith into the numerical world-class financial system. Boy, do we ever have a heated-up religious battle between the Bible and the business of Washington and the nation. Actually, there is no battle. It was decided long ago that the devotee lobbyist rules the politics. "Don't let the fiscal truth get in the way of your doctrine. Vote for Jesus!" or whoever their deity of worship is. In the meantime, watch your loot go out of your accounts into government trust.

Where was the faith-based movement during 2007-08? We sure could have used them. Maybe? I believe that this group may be late to the party. It's just clean up the trash time now. If they can. It's okay to have an educational effort to inform the public about matters of finance. But what good is learning about the basics of how a retirement plan works, for example, if the market has been blown to hell?

There were certain people preaching false prophecies who were leading the nation in positions of power when this disaster happened. I say, if you want to be a minister, don't run for political office. Please go and build yourself a church, so you can minister to your flock. Spare the general public the grief of listening to someone who has a position of political authority but wishes they were singing in the choir.

Bush himself said that he only listen to his God of his realization for advice and no one else. Now who prays to the same God as this man does? Because if you do and your God told him to make those careless and irresponsible decisions that he has damaged the nation with, then that should bring you great apprehension when siding with this man. Talk about faith-based economics. These administrations of the past and present will be glad to let you know that they put their allegiance to their God before the nations business. Once again I say to the citizens, look around at the remains. These results are also caused by a failed financial system of faith, believing that their way was the only way. This is not your run-of-the-mill religious ploy. They thought they could destroy the number system for their own gain and God would save it in the end. Seems like that's what went down.

This is my point. You must keep faith away from finance. Business and dogma don't mix. Repeat after me, class. "Business Has No Heart!" This is being demonstrated today for all the world to see. The number system is the number system, and the belief system is the belief system. Never the two shall meet. Now, how much simpler can I make it? We've not only had investment banks merging with commercial banks, which caused this disaster, but we've had this for many decades now and counting. Faith running finance has given us these claustrophobic consequences. I think it's time for churches to pay taxes, don't you? The joker politicians keep saying everyone should do their share to help get us out of this economic slavery; why shouldn't these organizations pay their fair share? Neither you nor I caused this scorched and dying financial earth. We still have to pay taxes, so what gives with the churches not paying?

The negative feedback loop of the Lord is in every facet of politics. It's having a devastating consequence on the laws and priorities of this nation. Since the church is so connected to the political lobbying efforts of this country, perhaps the churches should have to pay taxes to contribute a little more to reduce this economic turbulence. It's conceivable that if the church wards had been concentrating more on their official duties, instead of their personal yearnings, possibly we would not be on this terrifying road of no return.

You can't have a church if you don't have a nation. These believers who claim that their God is the one and only Savior is fine with me. I don't have a problem with that stance, generally speaking. They are basically indifferent toward a continuing search for where the knowledge and wisdom will lead them. Allow me to clarify my position. There are so many ancient books of wisdom, Dead Sea Scrolls and artifacts that coincide with the Bible, it's amazing that the church doesn't introduce more of this knowledge to its faithful. The believers could start a research group to prove that there are no other ancient wisdom teachings before or after the Good Book that are true.

I will never proclaim that I am some authority to listen to about a personal choice of belief influences. That's precisely my point, with some of these politicians and Wall Street leaders. They are doing the states' and the nation's business, but at the same time, they use their civic pulpits for spreading their dogmas. So, the country has in most cases elected a double agent. Some men or women of the cloth that are committed to their faith first. As I said, go build yourself a church and preach to your own Sunday congregation somewhere else. There's nothing wrong with that. Just go away and preach. You're wasting some good folks of the nation's time who want the nation's business done right!

Some people actually do wake up daily, believing they have the only true path to God. Many so-called "religitics" are allowing the creed of teamwork for the church first because of favoritism being put before the public needs. I guess they reason, who cares about their fundamentalism interfering with the nation's business? We are the nation's business. Well, just look around at the nation's business. What do you see that these fine, upstanding, say-so devotees have created for our future?

The sad thing is, it's their children's future also. Guess they forgot about that. A lot of these gospel opportunists who led us down this path were lost and oblivious. Sometimes this whole religious tenet has me thinking, are these people on some kind of a Jim Jones bender? We have to make sure that these jokers don't send us to Kingdom come—we will be done. I hope not. It's getting really close to us all being on suicide watch now, messing around with these shady characters.

These sanctimonious jellyfish power grabbers should use more caution in dodging the United States of America's pursuits of happiness. This is how things can get out of hand if you are not careful with the nation's business. We're facing possible extinction of the species, all for political egotistical games. Besides, who in the church is telling you about the economic story that I am leaving a record of? Either the religion is working on behalf of your families' well being, or it's working against your benefits. You have to decide that for yourself and yours. I'm just saying that the faith affiliation has a significant role in the fiscal fireworks of today. Once again, do some research.

A lot of good all the praying did for the citizens and the world during the Bush/Cheney administration, eight years in their power of destruction games. At least somebody got a job. They are still employed during speaking engagements! Maybe the Lord has led us down this road to financial madness. Not! Looks like the Satan in mankind has accomplished his mission. Thank the God of your heart, that there are many different paths to the mountaintop.

The empire didn't just die, it was murdered by people of a strong fake faith. At least they proclaim that they are devout believers. They somehow became lax in their responsibilities when it came to protecting the very citizens who elected them to be in positions of authority. I feel that, there's no way a person's faith that could have anything to do with the disintegration of the financial systems. Where was the Republicans' faith when their organized crime syndicate was breaking the international laws left and right? Did their faith have anything to do with billions of dollars squandered in the Middle East and the profits of the multinational corporations offshore bank accounts?

Who are we kidding? This is a hardcore material money bamboozle. This low form of non-regulation is nothing less than economic pornography. What's faith got to do with it? Their God would say to them if they would listen, don't blame your personal moral collapse on me. The power brokers won't listen anyway. If they did listen to their spiritual mentors, would we be in this mess now?

Yet, if you let some leaders tell you, they will say their faith led them to their decisions. I hope there's some wisdom in your faith that signals to you to protect the little guy. That's what got us into this financial smash-up we are currently suffering from. Not enough duty to the flag of the United States of America was in consideration. Then I say, there needs to be new leaders and they need a new faith. You tell me, what honorable person would use their belief system to cause conflict within themselves, within the nation and beyond? Not one in their right mind.

I am not a religious person, even though I was baptized and went to church until about the sixth grade, off and on. You didn't have to be religious to follow this financial hurting for the ages story. As a matter of fact, not many religious folks are even clued in on the current misery the world is facing today. Maybe the doctrine distracted many of the faithful. They meet often enough. Why didn't anyone see this economic communion of immorality coming? This collision travels across all boundaries of persuasion. If you're breathing, then you're affected by this Green Plague.

I can guarantee the pain in the wallet we are facing today is not an unseen mystery. It's been obvious since the days I started to pursue this reversed fortune of prosperity. With or without governments, economies can falter, as we are witnessing today. We can do bad by ourselves. We don't need these jokers to create any more letdowns in our lives. Eight years of hellish no-shows was just too much for this country to be able to sustain itself. We've been running on economic automatic power for decades now since before the end of the Clinton administration. But BushCo, along with the Street, raised the deficit chips to a level that allowed no one to stay and play in the fouled-up financial poker game. The whole system went kaput!

As time goes on, this episode in history of putting your blind faith into a supposedly saintlike leadership, will be judged to have been a farce! One grand financial and political power mirage. Just a super-stupid distraction looking back on it. Hell, I thought it was back then. Was this nation really that weak? Now, it seems that this once-great international symbol of freedom for the world is just one gigantic moral hazard black hole. Will we ever get out of this dollar bill bondage?

BushBama

The question of which president caused the recession, Bush or Obama, is actually a conversation not worth discussion to me, but I will in brief lay out the thesis for my statement. The reason I say this is, all you have to do is to simply just follow the facts. There aren't many arguments as to when the recession started. The official starting point the economists chose was December 2007. President Obama began his term in January 2009. The financial crash happened in 2008. Now, you do the math. It's all obstacles of eyewash to try to hide the bankrolling that went on from the same folks who are sending us all to the rock plies. The gossip debate about it is only a manifestation of the media.

The high officer of the land, Obama is dubious in his assumptions that he can fix the stock market, but the exchange was rocking and rolling long before he took office, believe me. He's repeating what the former prez did, but he has no choice. Everything he can do will still add zeroes to the national debt, and there is absolutely nothing he can do about that. He is a front man covering for the deficit creators. This creates uncertainty at best.

When President Obama came riding in on his white horse to save the day, I said to myself before he secured the rent-a-president gig, that he had no idea what he had gotten himself into. You could have elected God into office, and She could not get this mess straightened out that Rice and troupe left behind closed doors at the White House. Obama who? I felt like I was watching the American people's sacred cow being led to slaughter. I knew from years of examination of this big league market structural deficiency, that we were in new historic financial territory. Eight years of king-sized grief from the Bushwhackers and the Wall Street hackers was the lick that did the trick. They had brought down the public's home values here and abroad with fraud. The whole game of financial chicken was simply deranged.

My point is that Obama only had one shot to make any sense of his historic black presidency, in my opinion. That shot would entail distancing himself from the previous administration and claiming his time in the spotlight. Unfortunately, the opposite happened. Not only does he protect the Neo Con bulbs, but he had the nerve to be all huggy-kissy with "George W." on his special inauguration day. I said right at that moment, your term as leader of the free people is DOA. What he didn't know and respect is that the Bush gang, the Federal Reserve and the bankers left him and everyone else a good, old-fashioned out house of deficits to clean up: some 4 to 5 trillion dollars and counting from these good people of faith.

Put it this way. Obama was the perfect houseboy to clean up after eight years of a frat party gone insanely mad from these joy boys and girls. I keep saying to this day, when the hell is Obama going to get pissed off enough at the trash the last world leaders left for him to clean up after them? I mean, he can't begin to create his own presidential style because he is constantly locked in reverse trying to rectify his partners'-in-crime record. It ain't gonna work. He should be calling these guys for what they are. High-tone skunks. Kinda like he did in when he was on the campaign trail in 2008. Nope, not gonna happen. They're just one big sad family. You see why I'm a political atheist. Once again I vote for myself as my president. What representative can represent me better than me? I kept up with this economic green garbage, they didn't!

So, if Obama thinks he's fooling the investors, it ain't working. Never forget that while Obama was out there spitting his rhetoric to the masses on the campaign trail in 2008, I was watching Wall Street investors lose every confidence in Bush. I also watched them spit on his political carcass. Why is 'Obondsman,' I mean Obama's boy toy Bush, so important to the current prez? Why would he go to bat for a guy who left him hanging out high and dry? Maybe it's because if Obama does not keep up the spend-and-pretend game, the whole economic enchilada will come tumbling down faster than what the world is capable of dealing with. Obama didn't have the time to create this level of financial crimes.

Until due process of the unethical acts of these fake leaders are decreed in a court of law, the Universal laws will have to do for now. They are mankind's final hope. The Universal laws are also eternal and can never be modified by man. They will have to do to protect this planet and its inhabitants from the lawless lawyers. Why wait to see how the future will be when we primarily have only laws for the few at the top? We have no template for free enterprise unless all the laws of man are enforced. Particularly, you must arrest the oath takers in Washington and Wall Street. All we have is our word, and if that is no good, then we honestly do not have a representative government. Now is as good a time as ever to preserve the freedom for the children, so make up your mind, public politicos.

You can't put a wax shine on the financial floor until you sweep up the old dirt that's on the floor. Why would Obama, the Prez, remark that we will only look forward and not go backwards? I don't know about you, but it seems as though we are in all likelihood stuck in economic reverse, whether he realizes it or not. Now, if the current commander-in-chief can't see the dirt on the floor that was left by the last administration, then he has to have on blinders. I guess he never had to do chores at home when he was young. I know from having shared responsibilities at home if you were told to wax the floor, you had better not try to put a shine on that floor without first sweeping it clean, then mopping it and finally putting the wax shine on that floor. That's why none of the children would volunteer to clean the floors, because it was hard work. If our mother Sermeria caught us waxing the floor without sweeping it and mopping it first, we would get into big trouble. She knew that was a waste of time.

The same is true for America. Why ain't the world leader of the free world hiring people to clean America's floors the proper way? Usually it's the media's job to be the first to say that a nation should not look back to the last administration's years. It's very rare for a newly elected president to state categorically in so many words and non-actions, that if crimes were committed in the last administration, that is where they will stay. This ain't Las Vegas what I'm writing about here … or maybe it is. This is Real Street, where people are suffering extreme hardships. Sure kind of seems like Viva Las Wall Street, though. A very unsophisticated manner for the world's beacon of democracy to behave. No prosecutions for laws broken. Not very Shakespearian. That is really frightening!

The designers of this diabolical plot maybe don't want to stop the bleeding of the bloody empire. They would have good reason not to want it stopped. If the country stands again on solid ground, then a court of laws must be reinstated for the masses that will be prosecuted faithfully. That means no one is above the law. Well, here's the rub. Most of the standing federal politicos were on watch when many of the foul instigations were led by the statesman of ostrich descendants. They were very skilled at sticking their heads in the ground when backbone was needed to doubt and challenge the legislation in the past years of 2000-2008. So many have a lot to lose, including their lives in prison. Who wants to risk that happening? Why risk enforcing just laws at a time like this? They may be thinking, "So, you might as well let the whole game of the political and economical chaos go up in flames."

I'm not saying this way of thinking is going on and I ain't saying it ain't, but the way the lid is being kept on this story is something to behold. No big guns in the Bush administration inner circle, Wall Street or anywhere else in their top shop of monetary horrors are even in the loop for an investigation. This is some kind of a frightening key point of concern to watch. Only because if no one can be held accountable in a court of law, then this conspiracy from my lame brain at 2 o'clock in the morning, might have legs to walk or run with. It also could be that my writing this is just that, lame brain. Maybe? Time will be the best judge.

Alcohol as the Drug of Choice

I have a theory and it's one that I haven't thoroughly examined, but I know I'm in the game of scoring a goal with this one, so here goes. I noticed that whenever a society has alcohol as its number one beverage or drug of choice, their chances of becoming a thousand-year culture, or to be able to sustain the vision necessary for growth determination is exceedingly low because of eventual abuse of the system's laws. In other words, we need to dry out Washington and Wall Street! Let's create a dry county in their jurisdictions. I mean what are the guidelines for drinking with the government positions of importance?

It's been confirmed through the press that George W. was a major bottle fly from his late teens until around the age of forty. That's a ton of liquor. You've got to have some washed-out brain cells somewhere in your head from chugging that much moonshine. Looks like another power grab to put the family's name in lights is all that mattered. Maybe they wanted their names in the history books at all cost. Well, they made it. Only this time it's costing everyone. The headlines read: A financial washout happened on the Bush presidential watch!

Getting back to the stock exchange: The sky was the limit with the punch bowl drinking financial district. No one stopped to check whether the juice was spiked with derivatives. Seems like their motto was: "If the president serves up the drinks of no regulations, who are we to question the taste, even if it does destroy our economy?" How do we know we are not entrusting a bunch of guzzling intoxicated thirsty throats with our money on Wall Street and Washington? From the looks of things, we could be throwing our funds straight down the bottle. As a matter of fact, when looking back on it, does it not seem like we have just lived through some kind of alcoholic fiscal fog drunken stupor that has not lifted yet? What a hangover!

Feels like the world was run by drunkards. One thing is clear about boozers. They love to create violence. If there are no standards for supervising the most important finance system in the cosmos, why would anyone expect that there would be rules or guidelines on when and how much a politician or finance headman can chug the jug? Nobody's telling. Who's keeping score? Anyway, just thought I'd ring the alarm that's in the background of my mind. It could be pertinent only because those who make the decisions on the scales and weight of justice should be monitored in some way. Their bottle bravery should be kept to a minimum when voting. They could very well right now be making crucial decisions that will affect our lives for many years to come while being a little tipsy.

By the way, check the medicine cabinets of the officials also. I would add some protections for the voters that make public knowledge of the medication that the officials who are making decisions are taking. If you want the job, take a drug test, alcohol test and prescription confession. You agree? These judgments that the leaders are making will affect your kids' lives—and yours—for generations to come. I want to know what the hell pharmaceuticals they are digesting just before they are going to vote on some significant laws. Can this be done? I don't know, but it sounds good to me in theory. Put some pressure on these men and women to dry up, straighten up, and fly right!

Anything is better than what we have now. Remember the long drawn-out "War on Drugs" scam that the government misinformation trap convinced everyone to take notice of? Classifying pot the same as heroin. They were out of their freakin' overdosed minds. Anything the DEA could do to earn a buck, I guess, was justified in their distorted minds. A total failure. The war on drugs scam was so unsuccessful that the media does not even mention the phrase any more after twenty years of this disaster.

Now, all is quiet on the scene. They destroyed so many people's lives with this waste of time crap. This is important because these are the same people who are deciding your future with their lunatic laws. If this financial blowout was not alcohol induced, then that is really scary. You mean to tell me all this destruction caused by them was created while they were in a stable frame of mind? Wow! Say it ain't so. Why is it that the few smart lawmakers yield to so many dumb lawmakers? This has to stop!

Class Action Lawsuit

How can we ever correct this fiasco in our lives if we don't analyze who and what got us here? Well, it's because it took a lot rip-off artists that we have elected to get here. Some that we have not appointed to office, such as the Wall Street bunch. This is a financial guerilla war against the public, trying to send all of us to either some financial prison or worst. The repeat offender syndrome on Wall Street has turned this into a battle of the fittest. So far no one is willing to spill the beans on each other. Can you believe that? America's media is not taking names and leaving bodies in the streets of these outlaws who betrayed all of us. You want to take a guess as to why that would be and is?

Perhaps, when you delve into the story deeper you'll find that the media has been bought off a long time ago, the whole lot of them, what is commonly known as the mass media. The mass media is supposed to be the last bastion of truth to give the public an accurate detailed accounting, blow by blow of the latest important news. A charge of fraud by the solid citizens against their own government media sounds like a good idea.

A class action financial lawsuit against the U.S. government and Wall Street, for manipulating the free market system to an unfair advantage for the gain of the few at the top one percent and the pain for the many could be in order. What power does the citizen have to protect what's rightfully theirs? This process of economic roulette on the public has to be eliminated. The press must be given back to the population for our protection. If this keeps up, we all may be headed for the unemployment breadlines. Well, like I said earlier, one uncomfortable thought is that the Bush cabal will be gainfully hired by firms for large sums of money to speak about nothing of importance. At least these carpetbaggers who had a major role in creating this confusion will have a way to earn a paycheck for their family coffers. Nice work if you can get it. Over 15 million people out of work to date in the U.S. and counting. Can you believe the last leaders of the past high office are proud to announce their accomplishments at speaking engagements? Which world do these people really live in? One that I don't want to live in. It sounds like the Twilight Zone to me.

IX
PLAN B

THIS IS A ONE-OF-A-KIND EVENT. The planet's money system has never experienced anything like this before. The jewel of my information is not just about the monetary side of the discussion but the humanitarian part of the event. We only have one chance to get our lives back on the right track in managing our business and environmental world. There's no do-over on this bumma-drama! Now everyday is a new historic low. Records of finance are being shattered daily. The diamonds for me are in providing an effective vision for activating a mechanism of hope. I also want to give the reader an interactive template to assist in guiding them with words from the highest light of encouragement.

The Paradigm Shift

Make no mistake about it. There has been a paradigm shift in the rank and file economics of a dollar-dependant society. The expediency of deflation of the people's bank accounts is irreversible. I'm not just squawking about money, but the power shifting to the haves and the have-nots. The haves are reloading their funds as best they can. You as a money minion need to check and see what wrecked the wealth of the minions since most are included in that group. The ol' S.O.S.!

Well, it's a new day now. No longer do the empire's rulers have authoritative power over the people. Everyone sooner rather than later will catch on to their weak pretenses and laugh out loud at these buffoons. These political and monetary misfits that help close down the financial factory doors are fracturing dreams.

Then, they shut down the plumbing that cut off all of the integrity and ethics of the law that is supposed to flow through the pipes of justice for the purpose of earning the people's trust. The political and financial followers that were supposed to be the vanguard of leadership instantly lost all credibility in most eyes.

There's no time to waste with these senseless fantasies that got the ball of adversity rolling down on top of the communities in the first place. I'm speaking about the precedent of the world's greatest paradigm shift ever approaching. It's going to take a spiritual evolution to release us from these mundane habits of greed. There's a void that we are all witnessing, whether we realize it or not—a deep void of national leadership that has created an economic archetypal defect. We need leadership that can transform us now and point the way out of this pressure cooker. I'm speaking about a global consciousness conversion that is as drastic as when the horse and buggy gave way to the future of the automobile.

We must eliminate the present failed model of financial gain for the few and slim pickings for the multitudes. We cannot continue to travel down the wide path of dark demonic pitfalls that we currently face. What can point humanity toward the narrow path of truth and justice for all? Our collective commitment to the human race. The time is now to uplift yourself and everyone around you today. Not only will the masses regain a new vision of hope from despair, but the very vibration of the planet and the universe, for that matter, will transfer from systems of doom to a brighter point of view. What do you have to lose that you already haven't lost? Absolutely nothing! We need to make this move ASAP!

Why keep heading in the same direction we are today with the same old tired people who have already let you down? Everything they are leaving us is based on self-gratification and self-destruction. A world of meditative leaders with foresight and wisdom is the new paradigm shift that we must practice daily for most of the nation. Look, I can testify from the many years of investigating this money mirage of the stock exchange that this stuff is dull. A low vibratory nature. This whole breakdown is no wonder world of joy.

For a meditator seeking the higher spiritual realms of being, this financial game is a big, bad joke. How is it that this junk dominates so much of our lives? Everyone should realize that you can't take the material achievements with you when it's your time to return to your spiritual home. All of the scientific research today reports proudly, you will be a better individual and a healthier person if you meditate. You can help relieve some of the pressures on an outdated medical system at the least.

What good did all the companies' drug testing of employees at their job sites do as a contribution to the world? It created a ton of fear, and a lot of wonderful people lost their livelihood because of the flawed intentions of the bosses. Now, many more who took that damn stupid drug test are out of a job anyway. What was that? We know what it was and still is. Another drug scam for people to give up their rights to their bodily fluids to some losers at the top of the economic chain of pain. Perhaps the anti-drug enterprise system should have kept its eyes on the financial fundamentals of Wall Street. Instead, they were overly concerned with what people were doing in the privacy of their homes. Another crazy, unsustainable brain-dead drug prohibition failure, any way you measure it.

We as a people will not be used any more as only a data storage dump for their press corps to politicize and hide the mistakes of the elites. As long as we have the same clowns that caused the debacle running the show, then the shift is delayed and the success of our mission is also postponed. We can't wait any longer. Tell these bad actors to just go away. Nobody respects them anymore. The time is now for the new visionaries, the ones who are truly interested in building a sustainable society for all to share the resources, as they did in the labor to create those goods. Not the current model of the few at the top who are content to destroy the public goodwill. This is imperative that we must correct this mode of operation.

This next change might seem frivolous to a nonspiritual person who is dominated primarily by the body and fame, but if we can go out in the world and do one nice thing for a stranger that's down on their luck, this can go a long way to fixing the world's problems. I know it sounds too small of a measure to make a difference in the world, but from experience, I've witnessed the miracles that can be activated through acts of kindness. Changing from a selfish nation to a selfless nation.

This is just the beginning of the directional changes I envisioned that will help partner us out of the woods of enemy fire. With the energies to pull ourselves up by our bootstraps and start a process of rejuvenation that's good for the galactic system, we are allowed to build a cosmic cocoon of stability. Along with hope and wisdom, may we never approach this terrorized anxiety created by these monsters of mismanagement of the republic's treasuries again.

I know that I am not what you might call an orthodox author, but I never thought I would be writing a book on this intimidating cock-and-bull story anyway. Here's another one of my remedies for what's ailing the economy. If we could just stop letting the school kids only learn the basic education that I learned forty years ago, we would go a long way in manifesting a new breed of creature. A forerunner of pioneering principals that would make our educational ideology of today look like the backwoods routine that it is. It is a quantum world of existence now. Quantum beings. QBs. We must have an awareness of our divine connection to every light energy that has and still exists from all times before and today. The fifth force.

There's no going back to the older model. That's where our troubles begin and end. The child of the current times needs to examine their conscious ability and not just their physical and mental abilities. This is of the utmost importance. What we are talking about here is the invention of an upgraded DNA evolved child of a higher natured being. I'm talking about no less than a species switch turning on and lighting up the awareness of a cutting-edge schoolchild.

The accepted outdated thought trance model of just cracking the books open is not adequate anymore. A refreshing inner sensing design of a prototype creature that the world has never seen as a collective, particularly, the western cultures with its rigid domination of rules and laws that chokes off creativity. They would no longer live in patterns of confinement paying attention to a driven review and comparison of their lives. We need a child that loves to explore the meaning of life. One that can be taught to reflect, not just their outer world, but their inner answers also.

This gives them a distinct advantage over the rest of the classes in the world of materialistic studies and consequences. We can start today. You can tap into your power within your hall of records. It is always greater than the power that is outside of you. The superiority of the prince and princess of brightness will be of a great benefit to the forces of goodness. Let the ceremony of the purposeful quantum student being commence. The QSBs have arrived.

Here's a couple of more changes that I see would help humanity lift its outlook on life. We can raise the planets' vibratory frequency if tomorrow, instead of the children pledging their allegiance to a nation-state that has no concern for them, perhaps the kids could devote themselves to healing our planet by promoting an awareness of inspiration through a morning ceremony, lead by a Shaman of the earth or some other kind of naturalist that's attuned with Mother Gaia, as the ancient Greeks called our planet.

Forget about the mundane nation's flag only. Salute a higher, more eternal flag of galactic proportion. The bottom line is that without our nature rock Earth, no one will be going to school any more if circumstances continue unabated as they presently stand. So, what do you have to lose to try something radically different? Who cares if the kids know about Columbus discovering America right now? We can investigate that at a time when that's important to a nation's survival.

Right now we need to save the planet, the kids, and the wildlife. That is top priority. Conceivably, with the Earth child angels sending their love and gratitude out in harmonic unison, we can create a key component to assisting all of humanity to succeed. A simple mantra said daily by the young souls could give us permission to join the Federation of Peace. If there is such an organization of supreme reclassification for mankind, we need to move ahead full force and locate the headquarters. If not, the planet needs to create its own peace union. Sounds good to me.

For example, the young minds could recite these words of cooperation in morning class daily: "Great living planet of all life forms. Make of us an instrument of service for the lifting of humanity and the healing of the world. May we speak truth within ourselves and to any individual we meet on our path. Know that all people are one family, one life, on the threshold of a new understanding of our existence. Preserve and respect the animal and plant kingdoms for all future generations to treasure. So it is done!" Why not try this? Look at the schools' conditions today. It might do some good. Tell the teachers and administrators that you read about this concept in this book, and you are ready to make a change that can make for a better student. About five minutes a day to help our planet is not a lot to ask. I can guarantee you that the present corporate enterprise government gave up on the kids a long time ago.

No Fault of Joe and Jane Public

Not just anyone is going to pick up a book with a title like this. So I commend you on continuing your search for the actuality of what is happening in the financial markets of madness. Right now the people of the empire are feeling down in the dumps, disheartened, and their psychology is disoriented. Humans are critters of habit that are also going to sense the cyclic changes of our planet as well as a ripping of the fabric of the world's legal tender. We are symbiotic creatures, programmed for all of our lives from birth to express the importance of the nation's currency. There's no way not to become discouraged. We're looking at the possibility of living in a world with little to no opportunity to use the very tangible assets that most went to a higher educational learning institution to gain. A job skill, so that you could earn the best chance of increasing your odds that you will be able to collect your fair share of greenbacks to assist in solidifying your destiny.

Now, the vision to earn your dream living is evaporating at a rapid pace. That is an extremely depressing thought. Your mind can't accept the likelihood of you becoming a liability and can't pay your monthly obligations. Especially since you played along with the system like a good soldier and still got destroyed! The bill collector is not happy about this prospect, either. We generally want to do the right thing as citizens. Individuals try to pay their cost of living expenses because we face the reality that, you can't get something for nothing. The opposite of the way Wall Street mentally works.

Personally, most of the folks that I know are not trying to heist the taxman, even though many privately scream that the taxman is trying to burn the citizenry. Tell me, what do you do when the economic charlatans have deliberately restricted your capacity to be gainfully employed by disintegrating the economy? Their choice, not ours! Now the question is, must we accept a never-ending financial system of errors as our future economic plight in our short lives?

Our cleverness and inventiveness as an educated public is our country's number one asset. With ingenuity and attention to details, the American worker is as fine a thinker, creator and laborer as you can find qualified anywhere on the planet. We deserved better political and financial representation. Why should we have our entire endowment to command a living by having an expertise be comprised? The system itself is not the problem. It's the lower nature of human limitations, incompetence, and clumsiness that brought on this downfall. The world monetary methodology has a pattern of fixed fiscal disarray and official mismanagement. Translation: "We've been had! The establishment has failed us!"

It is not the time to listen to those who don't know. There are many of them from the last decade still around flapping their big fat lips and don't know what they are talking about. That's how we got here. Their words are as dead as the skin that the snake sheds and leaves behind to perish in the sands. Life has shed the old model of being only a materialist. We must not become that dead skin that these past and current administrations are financially obligating us to be. We certainly need a new form of energy and vitality. Some beings where their wisdom and knowledge have moved beyond the parameters of church and state.

What is required is some new wave energy being. Not just a particle being controlled only by the boundaries of the body. We must abandon just having desires predominantly for possessions of personal gains. Your inner strength is what you're going to need in the near future to survive. That is the only security that we truly can direct for our best outcomes.

Not Good Stewards of the Planet

Wow, it seems like ages since the U.S. resources were not mostly used for the production play of a war in the Middle Eastern theaters. All the while these combat junkies didn't have a notion of another war which was brewing, and that was much more significant than the minute man enlisted effort. It's fair to proclaim that the other war they should have been foreseeing is against none other than that adorable foe herself, Mother Earth. She's not usually this angry, but mankind has tipped the scales of imbalance on the planet. So much so that unless the Earth rises up and take a swipe at the unaware pupils of the planet, how will the elected officials know when to stop breaking laws?

Before all of this fiscal and monetary mess broke out, I was in the process of writing a book on climate change in 2006. Really. It is one of my most concerning topics that was and still is in my life. I realized recently that when I came across the beginning of my climate book, this stock market eruption had swept me up. I had time lost somewhere while checking in on these money matters. I could not believe that for five years I had not gotten back to continuing on my path with my atmospheric book. That's a blowmind for me, all by itself. That just shows me that this Wall Street and past White House budget deficit thang is really a big bang event. The funny thing is that I'm only writing about the tip of the iceberg when it comes to this economic reversal.

We as a species have not been good stewards of our planet. This world is on loan to us from our Creator. There's no doubt about it. The planet is not our enemy. We are our own worst enemies. We as humans can do bad with no help from the planet! Just look around today. It took billions of years to create the heavenly environment and the atoms that we enjoy presently. Yet, many treat our very lifeline of civilization, the Earth, as though it is some type of a cheap subprime loan. That's stating it mildly.

The Bush administration's disasters certainly extend into the climate change arena. These questionable, self-centered, time-wasting people did not make it really clear that they were aware that part of their responsibilities was to create laws that protected the Earth's atmosphere for future generations. These bulbs at times could only see, it seems, as far as their buttholes, which is where they kept brains stationed in park. The Wall Street heads were not any better. These jet-setting renegades, traversing the planet spewing pollutants out of their jet planes and out of their credit default swaps, which they spread and sold around internationally, delivered a knockout blow to humanity's system of finance ... and maybe the planet.

I need to clarify the problem. We're helping to create the unsustainability on our only extraterrestrial prize. It's not so much anymore about the things we buy in this economy. It's more so about the awareness we bring into the natural arena of nature. We must assist our rock in ways of gratitude, meditation, prayer, visionary insights, and any other methodology you wish for boosting the immune system of our planet. Do it! We all can't be fighters; someone has to do the quiet, inner work to help out. That works, too.

We are traversing space on this craft Earth at about 300,000 mph—that's what the scientists say. Traveling about eleven million miles a day around the Milky Way Galaxy. Then, for the life of me, answer me this. If our spherical life support system, the Earth is a spacecraft speeding across time and space, why can't we be classified as extraterrestrial beings? We live on a rock that is never in the same place in time. I just made a proclamation. Human heredity is of an unknown origin from other worlds. There! I said it! You go, you ET! Just a sighting I had.

Before I got on my small ET tangent, I was going to examine the climate in more details. First, let me state that I've been monitoring the world climate for almost 15 years now. I've seen Earth changes back then that happened when there was not much of a conversation about this topic. In about 1997, when many people were glued to the TV screens, watching Bill Clinton's impeachment trials, I had my eye on the sparrow, Earth's climate!

There would be days that are just like now with this economic bomb going off. I would be falling out of my chair, the reporting was so alarming about our atmosphere. That lonely feeling came over me because once again who wanted talk about the peat bogs, or the jet stream, or the dead zones in the ocean or about breakaway floating icebergs back during those times. Not many, if any. You may be questioning why I'm giving you this brief history of my climate observational past. That is because I'm attempting to qualify my coming criticisms and considerations when elaborating on this subject.

It is a time of truth-seeking for stern and devoted servants that will qualify for the changes and challenges that lie ahead. During the era of rejection for planet assistance, little to no funds went into the environmental coffers compared to the military machine of high esteem. Their invasions still have a vibratory pattern of sadness for our planet. No one would or could stop these monsters without causing bodily harm to themselves. We should have treated them like the animals they are. Their front men and women at all the agencies kept the regulators at bay from attacking them, including and especially certain elements of the media that stood guard, blocking off any insults these depraved beasts deserved.

I know this may sound like harsh language, but you have to remember this global climate change is a long and tedious journey for me. I'm screaming about preserving our lifeline. You should be openly upset, too, that the mismanagement of our Earth's resources might jeopardize our very existence. Meanwhile, our planet is taking a course of its own for the worst. Very few in this crack house for power addicts are cognizant of the oncoming climatological trends. The world is about to change a trillion times over.

The surroundings of a clash of warriors in man's wars are not a pretty exhibition, but it pales by comparison to a clash of climate patterns in the world. A manmade war is child's play. When it comes to making a choice between, do we go to war or do we work on saving the planet? Save the planet! Without the Earth, who cares about you displaying your devastating fields of bloodshed? Moving ahead because of mismanagement at the top of the chain of command, there are multiple climatic disruptions in the near firing line because of failed targets. I guess it's just our bad luck. We got the worst of the worst as far as the guardians of the gates who were supposed to be protecting our pretty planet. Now not only is this country getting ecologically attacked, so is our planet.

Still, the planet gives us beautiful sunsets and moonrises—they are to live for. If we want these inspiring attributes of the Earth to continue, we all had better work together. Fast and soon. The government must transform itself from a materialistic body of rules to a meta-governing body of inner perspectives and wisdom. An alternative approach of holding hearts with other nations before holding and shaking hands would be helpful. A world where gaining all the wealth in the stratosphere is not the goal. Having a healthy populace that is contributing to the well being of all humanhood is a higher purpose. We're tired of the old policy of only the few at the top shall share in the riches. Look at the disaster that is brewing using this system!

Just like any person in the world, if you don't have your health, you ain't got nothing. So is this true of a nation and especially our pre-eminent planet. The animals and the human animals are a surefire symptom indicator as to how the terrestrial sphere and empire are doing. If the citizens are down in the dumps, so too is the globe and nation of those people. It always goes back to that old theme: The leaders must either lead or get the hell out of the way, and let some qualified folks get in there and clean up this outhouse. Here are two technological suggestions that might work to our environment's advantage and assist in saving the day.

Terra preta is a bio-charcoal process I read about a few years ago; you will have to do your own research on the internet because it's difficult to explain. The next is a product called Bucky paper, which is a kind of nanotechnology material. Once you take the liberty to do due diligence on this topic, you will find there are some solutions to our climate woes if the war regime will get out of our planet's way. Just to let you know I am not just a whiner about the climate, I'm giving you some qualified solutions that could possible transform the planet and take some of the high CO2 risk out of the atmosphere and bring into balance a more stable environment.

OK. Some of you might be saying, it ain't no freakin' event such as global warming. It's an atmospheric solar system change, not just a climate change. I know that it's all well connected. It's also true that the collective solar system is the template for our planet of earth changes. I can agree with that thesis about the solar system's climate influences. After all, when you're dealing with a subject this extensive, you must allow room for other qualified theories. One thing I do know is that I don't know everything and never claimed to know everything. Quite frankly, I glad I don't know all there is to because that would leave me no more questions to ponder in the future. That would be so sad for me, mentally speaking.

All I'm really saying is that mankind should tighten up its environmental regulations for the good of the entire planet, solar system, galaxy, multiple universes, and all of existence. Seems like this entire book is about protecting what we got or had. Whether it be the laws of this nation or a climate, an above-board administrative buffer is required for the safekeeping of a young blooming republic. What happens to that civilization is not the question that should describe our fate. If we as a species choose not to rectify our imminent direction to Downerville, oncoming generations will always have to wonder, "What were they thinking?" That advanced culture of the New Millennium.

A lot of not-so-bright people did hold top important executive positions in the legislature of the greatest free democracy in the world. I know that might seem like small potatoes to some, but you might want to make a little note of that fact of life. Like I say, the numbers state the facts. The climate is nothing to mess around with. It's a colossal bubble bursting now. It's happening already. The evidence is everywhere. These creature politicians let everything get out of control here on our lifeline, Earth. By being more concerned about wanting to be seen as liberators of the Middle East than our natural environment they did a two for one. They ended up with neither one of our environments on solid ground, ecologically speaking. The big blowback is in full effect mode now.

People are freaking out everywhere now about their local weather. Hell, it's so bad as far as the climate change is concerned that even these non-insightful politicians are showing signs of apprehension. Not! "Everything is perfectly calm," exclaim the bulbs. Yeah, right! I knew these invasions would come back to bite each and every one of us on multiple levels. Even a blind person could see that coming. Some have blindness from physical challenges, and others have the condition known as a blind mind that can't see. The "Yes We Can!" slogan platform that President

Obama campaigned on was nothing more than spitting in the wind. The catchphrase should have been, "Will We Change?" So far nothing has, but our climate has in a major way!

They rose again to their standard of underachievers. The climate is at a major crossroads, and these people added to the misery of Mother Earth by setting off new world bombs in foreign lands, pretending to be some kind of desktop G.I. Joes, never entering the field of battle that they waged on the planet. Look around at the conditions of our atmosphere at this late date, and tell me there are no issues to be overly upset about. Now there's so much that has to go perfectly for humanity to prevail above the current downfall of climatic, economic, and social conditions. It's going to take a superhuman effort just to survive these miscalculations.

Here's a theory of mine from my feeble brain that's drained. If the planet is a living entity as many ancient cultures have claimed that it is, then the planet could be seeking a request to have the pretentious destroyers of our climate investigated. This could be a mandatory demand from our rock of joy, Earth. Those with intuition to sense the atmospheric signals are aware of this. In order to right the wrongs of the unenlightened dignitaries, a call for quick justice is necessary for the neglect of their climatic duties. We as denizens are being asked to make a choice between protecting the policies of the short-sighted hoods who allowed this Earth's compromising faith that we are currently experiencing, or to not do anything.

The result of doing zero about this political alienation is the equivalent of surrendering to a band of combatants. If that was to happen, there would be a worldwide crying of the dream creatures, us. We must strike a balance and save our Earth rock of hope for all of the next generations of species to come. May we never again have to make a decision because of political follies between preserving our lives or choosing planetary annihilation. These inferior bureaucratics cannot save us. We the people are the true treasures of this nation. We must rescue ourselves!

What Will Be, Will Be

Once again, I knew that my research of the ancient prophecies predicted that our present evolution is a very important time in mankind's conscious development. Many prophecies have declared that the future is not written in stone; instead, it is left open to a multitude of potential possibilities. It's a gray area. Depending on how mankind interprets the coming times will determine how well off we will be. So did we choose wisely? Our children, the wildlife, and every species' existence depend on it.

Well, with the start of the war in Afghanistan and then Iraq, the nation shifted its direction. Wall Street early on was taking their lead from Washington. They had no hesitation in letting the floodgates of sucker bets pervade the economic landscape. Greed abounded. I'm writing this information hopefully to let more people know that the world has not ended yet, but it could change drastically if we don't get in tune with our intuition of having a higher purpose for your life plan than just what you experience in your objective life.

We are approaching the year 2012, which is marking the end of a 26,000-year Precession of the Equinoxes cycle. The ancient Mayan culture long ago predicted that this eternal cycle would conclude in our lifetime. The anthropomorphic creature has never witnessed such an event, or non-event as some speculate. We are here on planet Earth at this very profound and sacred time in mankind's history because we all are divine. We are the chosen beings to enter a new and exciting gateway or portal. This will shift our species into a new great cycle beginning from the start but also end of an epic period in humanity's history.

The Creator, who has placed us on this planet during this cycle of events, had a purpose for us the guardians to have more of a galactic concern. The Bible says God is light. The light source of the universe knows you're quite capable of answering the call of the mythical duties that is being demanded from you right now. Acknowledge your place in galactic history for this current moment. Be present. Forget about the frivolous politics and episodes in your life at this time in mankind's history. This occurrence is greater than any childish vision of bogus bank accounts or war games. This is truly about peace games.

A great psychic energy is pervading the cosmos at this time in our lives. Learn all you can about this larger-than-life spectacle that is coming down as I write this book. The ancient cultures all say that the way we live our mortal lives will determine how we will live our eternal lives. The fact that we are entering into a new cycle of age that is truly building up an anticipation for those who know is awe-inspiring all by itself.

What will happen in 2012, exactly? No one has ever been through a cycle of this magnitude before, so all bets are off. There are no conclusive answers, but I will speak about what some are saying that are very qualified, as opposed to misguided buffoons. Many uninformed opinions were thrown up against the wall. First, let me state that so far, one of the aspects of the 26,000-year cycle is that the Earth and the Sun will align with the center of the Milky Way Galaxy at precisely 11:11 on December 21, 2012. This is called the Great Precession or the Dark Rift. We are in this window of time right now! The cycle has begun.

There are three camps of visions for this time we're approaching fast. Camp A says that nothing will happen and everyone will wake up on December 21, 2012, and carry on with their day as they normally would do. Camp B says that all hell will break out, and there will be world destruction and pole shifts as we enter this new age. Camp C says that speaking from a hyper-dimensional perspective, we as divine humans are part of the spacecraft Earth, and all of universal existence. The ancient mystery schools teach that if we as species can raise our vibratory frequencies within ourselves through meditation, we can not only save our spacecraft, but also preserve the planet's life for the animals and plants. It's imperative that you only listen to those who knows about this topic and do your own research.

As of November 2009, the government has come out with its own version of the events that will occur during the December 21, 2012, date of concern. A movie spectacular called "2012" was just released as I wrote this book. I've been wise to the 2012 event since I first learned about it in 1993. I came across a radio show called The Art Bell Show, and my life has never been the same since. Thanks, Art, for the knowledge and astuteness you and your guests turn the seekers of new visions onto. You gave us the courage back in those early days to know there were many light workers with a similar mindset and passion for leaving no stone unturned when it came to chasing the light wisdom. The show was informative and a trend setter. Of course, the show was hosted by its creator Art, and that gave the listener a genuine experience. Today the show is called Coast to Coast AM. It is hosted by George Noory, and they have continued to present a quality show. Keep up the good work.

My point is that I've heard and seen many experts in the 1990s and the new century speaking on the topic of 2012. I also have read many books on this subject. Each author/researcher has brought a unique vision to the table about the subject of 2012. At no time do I remember a discussion of what did the government know about the 2012 event. It just was not an important element of the purpose of the mystery. This is a universal supernatural actuality ... not manmade. Why, after all these years, would the government make a propaganda movie about this time in history? If the government really knew and could interpret the true purpose about 2012, they would not be creating wars on multiple fronts on our planet at this time with this life-changing cycle approaching at warp speed.

They either are fools for starting bogus wars if Judgment Day is coming, or you don't realize your sentence will be pronounced soon for the life you have led. I can't think of one national politician that I would consider an expert on the subject of 2012. From everything that I understand that the experts are saying, this is exactly the time for the opposite of what the budget busters are doing. This is a time for peace and self soul reflection, which is a far cry from the beating of the war drums.

We should be getting ready for this once-in-a-lifetime change as a nation and the leadership doesn't have a clue. As usual, the boys in the black suits missed the entire meaning of 2012. This is not surprising. Once again, these are the same so-called distinguished masters of the bankroll that missed the complete financial recession that started in December 2007 officially being announced in December 2008 that it had started the December before. If the executive branch missed the beginnings of the economic breakdown that they had a major part is causing, you tell me, how are these legislative bureaucracies going to make the call on a 26,000-year cycle? Logic says there is no way. We are on our own. As in the hit piece movie "2012," all the policy regulators are content to do is to blow things up and scare the public.

The real story about 2012 is a much more enlightened epic. There is no movie that could ever do it justice. The TV is just TV, and a movie is just cinema. Both are giving a depiction of an event through the eyes of a modern mortal. The movie is reality cinema at its best. The figment of someone's imagination of how 2012 could happen will never come close to the everlasting life-changing circumstances beyond our control that is in motion in the cosmos as I pen this book. It's coming to a real live theater near all species of the earth and beyond, soon. The ancient wisdom that's at the center of this beautiful epoch is so stunning and mysterious, that until this day, no one knows exactly what's coming down through the Milky Way Galaxy to present a gift to all of humanity. So don't be sold a bill of goods again that the inept powers of society know a damn thing about the true meaning of 2012.

Either way, they are entering a spectrum of order that will have them to answer for their deeds, as we all will. I would not want be in their shoes of misused authority right now. It all goes back to the question of honor. Do you choose the money while you are in a supervisory command of the empire, or is it glory that's your cup of tea? Leaders must truly devote their lives to making a positive contribution to their oath and to humanity. Most take the bait and choose the money and fame. Why not? Wall Street is just a handout away. What an empty shadow of wasted beings.

Now the glory guys and gals can take their good deeds with them when it's their time to check out! Since we don't know the right answer of what's going to happen in 2012, it's better to be safe than sorry. So my advice to you would be to start a program of meditation immediately. Not for me, but for your own soul and the uplifting of humanity. You don't have to discontinue your religion. I've met many mystics that are also members of a certain dogmatic faith. If nothing else, this is a small feat to develop to help you through these doubtful times. Besides, the doctor says it's good for your health.

No Magic Pill

I know that some of the things I'm writing about are too grand to get your mind around. For me, too. In this field you have got to throw some conspiratorial concepts against the wall of Wallshington Street. There's no hub of informational data to let you know whether you are moving in the right direction or not. This is a new and fresh financial crash event. Show me any of the elites that have the clear course of action to take when it comes to dissecting and correcting this entangled fictional numbers exchange. At least with folks offering conspiracy ideas maybe some of them are right and can help us to recognize the dangers that are approaching us at a fast rate. Besides, what has been offered so far by the government as the reasons for this global financial collapse?

They only have some facts alone with speculations also. I just don't understand why do some U.S. agencies freak out when the citizens are searching for the truth? Of course, the individuals who were in power when the loosey-goosey dollar bills were being printed don't want their names mentioned in connection with this economic show-stopper. These fiscal issues could not be this dire, you might say, but this is where the data has led me to so far in my travels. So arrest me for trying to understand the breakdown of the world's premier global economic system. Some folks wanna shoot me for being concerned for my country. I guess they possess some better answers than I have as to why we are in this monetary mess.

Put up the information or shut up. Why is it that they get to express their views wherever they wish to with no fear of retaliation, while someone such as myself who broke no laws but broke my ass looking for the secrets of the system disruptions that I didn't know existed can get sweated by the protectors of the creators of this mayhem? Wall Street, land of the free-debt slaves.

Some of this is heartbreaking to hear, and other parts of this book can bring you hope. It's all coming from my heart and not just my head. Boy, during my migration through the wilderness of Weird Street and beyond, there sure have been some doozy stories to take note of. For instance, the one about the international currency war between the Swiss banks and the IRS concerning the accounting and tax evading procedures of offshore banking accounts. Then there's the infamous "Credit Crunch" itself that brought down multiple corporations to their knees. There was Bear Stearns, Lehman Brothers, Countrywide, AIG, Fannie and Freddie, General Motors, and many more.

Now the media only wants to write and speak about the economic troubles of 2008-09, forgetting about the summer of 2007 market dislocation. Take this advice from an economic crash vet that it's of paramount importance to not shortchange the Credit Crunch itself. This is not a wise thing to do. This is the event that set the financial falldown of Wall Street into motion. Perhaps because the correspondents missed the Credit Crunch when it was happening, they can't really comprehend the pain it caused and its importance to our everyday existence. The lifestyle of what the average Joe and Jo Ann deals with daily will be a thing of the past because of these companies' behavior that caused this financial freeze-up.

I do believe some form of mankind will survive, but not in its current shape. We are already living a different lifestyle today than we were just a couple of years ago. Already the present attributes of the market have changed forever. Who is it that expects the market to return to the glory days of 14K any time soon? Only an idiot would speak those words. Oh, the Federal Reserve said that the market was showing signs of recovery in the fall of 2009. The recovery will be long and slow for generations to come. There's no magic pill.

They want you to believe there is. To be honest, even after all the study I have done on this subject, I still don't have an answer as to how do we get out of this mess. Still in some strange way, I have hope. I just can't accept the fact that modern man has concocted a way to destroy humanity through a complex financial shape-shifting process. Say it ain't so! Become aware and prepare is the motto of the day. Prepare, not only like you would in an emergency event, but also a non-standard prolonged emergency, maybe for years of change. Maybe forever!

Even on the stock market, the Wall Street executives missed the event themselves. Talking about being the mouse in the cat's ear! They were right in the mix and were inattentive to future disruptions because many of them were caught up in the political rhetoric. Don't feel so bad for yourself not to know that you were scammed. There were major media operations telling you how to think. Wall Street surely thought we were in the Golden Age listening to the CNBC network nonsense in 2008. That's a sad commentary all by itself. Now, we are all just witnessing the aftereffects from the mismanagement of the people's and the nation's treasures.

If we could just recover the debt created by the Bush conservative administration of close to five trillion dollars-plus off of the nation's books, we could for sure eliminate most of America's immediate financial problems. What did we get as citizens for spending that outrageous amount of money anyway? A big fat ZIP! Zero! Nada! The fat middle finger of finance!

I'd like to say that the journey for me of this critical fiscal observation situation is a period of my life that can never be compared to anything I've witnessed before. It's no time to relax. A slow-passing iceberg of fiscal danger is moving ahead. It's time to pay attention, people, more than ever before in your life. Now I truly feel in my gut that my whole physical life has been a scam to some degree. Trying to get to the so-called top of society is a delusional myth. There is no top or no bottom. Only the degrees of instant utopia for the haves and dashed hopes for have-nots. They are all brought to you on behalf of the grand illusional competitive committee. The game's rules are simple. Now you have it. Now you don't! The poverty game!

Whether you want to be a contestant or not, you or someone you know will be participating in this life game. We are all being choked by the financial smother-your-brother need for greed. We are directly interconnected to the wheels of deals. Give a contestant on a game show a wad of money and witness the elation and gratitude they express at that moment. What about a lottery winner? You could not find a happier person on the planet at that time. We are the money and the money is us, in most cases. That's the way we as citizens were trained. Now the retraining begins.

Still, I know in my soul that there are silent workers of the light, assisting mankind. I always tell people there are more good people in the world than bad, because if there were a greater number of individuals with traits of non-morality and questionable character, then the world would not survive the barrage of senseless humans bent on going bad. It would just be too many occasions for wrong things to happen to good folks. So, thank goodness that most people are decent.

If we could just get back to networking with nature, while strolling and looking at the leaves on the trees. Watch the birds go by. Nature has always had answers to our greatest concerns. We might just pull through as a species if we can find our way back to a simpler lifestyle of comfort and happiness. There is always the cherished reward of the higher light being improving your chances for success. When you are fighting for saving that bit of blue sky, you have always got a chance to be victorious. Fight for the right!

Look, I have been following these specific tracks of the economic blowout as far back as four years ago. If anybody wants to see a light at the end of the tunnel of this fiscal neglect, it's me. It's just that so far, well, I'm seeing a light at the end of the tunnel coming toward us. I'm just wondering, does the light have a train of friendship or a foe connected to it? In some weird way, I still don't get why we have to go through this. For what and for who are the questions. We can all guess on the what and the who, but I still just don't want to go down those churning economic drain train tracks. Will we learn our lessons? Probably not.

We are knocking on the door again. What door, you might ask? The door that was left open by the nation's economic debt promise to pay back obligations going up in flames. Not worth the cyber-security note it was intended to be. The leadership is programmed to drive the economy into Great Depression territory again, I guess. One lesson to learn from this book is that these same political people who landed us on the sinking island of finance do not deserve to manage neither the nation's nor your budget. That's an understatement!

Making the Call

Can the Greater Depression really be detoured? Mankind's fiscal downfall has opened up a wormhole that is revealing many future challenges for those with eyes to see. The pressure is on. One effort that you can engage in to help yourself is to do your own research and listen to those who do know. There are a few around. Even if you don't get clued in to someone else, this information in this book can give you a good idea of where the economy has been during the past decade, where it is now and where it is possibly going. I can only tell you my best educated perceived version of the shakedown. On October 31, 2009, the Dow Jones finished down 250 points. In my eyes the stock crashed in the spring of 2008. The Lehman Brothers meltdown was just the result of the earlier 2008 crash, in my opinion. Still today, I feel like a doctor diagnosing their patient. I could see clearly what were the precise ailments of the financial runaway economic train of pain. Just call me Dr. Johnson. Self-educated by a new course in the University of Financial Crashes.

What a Plan B is all about, in my limited view, is having a spiritual security first. Know that some American Indians believed we could never perish. Our soul just moves on to another part of the river of life. Therefore you just have to train and trust your inner strength. Your temple within. I often tell my wife that if anyone has a right to be depressed about this junk trunk of derivatives, it's me. Yet, I still manage to put on a happy face most of the time. It ain't easy always thinking ahead. Trying to estimate when the next big bust is going to happen and whether this is the final straw. Hell, it's all a gut check and a gut call now. I'm just trying to see the overall pattern of this commercial volcano spouting off plumes of insecurity.

That's where the experience of pain comes into play. I feel fairly confident through experience, that I can make an overall call on this fiscal end result. Me writing this book should be some kind of clue. Not many people of any color, race, or religion can pen a book on this massive event topic and actually have something to contribute for the betterment of society. I guess we'll see whether I was right or wrong on my calls. Once again, I'm justifying my lead-in to my next paragraph. I'm no voodoo accounting master like Wall Street is. I'm just a simple citizen trying to follow the circumstances that has caused perhaps the termination of the free market capital system of the world's superpower engine, America. Unfortunately, one day, all families will be discussing this bewildering subject matter.

Where do I begin? Maybe at the end. Like I have been saying all along in this book, a tremendous amount of dollar destruction consequences are headed our way. There is nothing we can do about it at this late date. The Federal Reserve printing dollars like they are going out of style. Guess what? The greenback is going out of style. Its present value as I pen these words is at a fourteen-year low. I'm not going to get into the deflation vs. inflation debate. Just know we're standing on shaky economic footing. What

I would advise your family to do first is to gather as much knowledge about this happenstance as possible. As you become more informed, more people around you can enhance their enlightened perceptions. This improves your survival chances by increasing your knowledge and discussions. Sometimes I see no way out of the dense monetary stupidity that led us all down this destiny of doom path. The collective integrity of the truthfulness of the human species as a race is in jeopardy. We still have a part to play in this entire play of life.

As I wrote previously, for the short-term gain of a few we all must pay the cost. There is really not enough constant conversation about this event. Not enough people know how to deal with this shakedown. Just telling your family that life as we once knew it has changed forever is enough to blow anybody's mind. What does that all mean? It means that your basic way of life can be no more. A breakdown at the top of governments also activates a breakdown at the bottom levels of civilizations. Yes, it's true. I'm searching for the words to say that because of the negligence of financial world's leadership, your family's course of life will change. No doubt about it. I hope for all humanity's sake that I am wrong. Sorry to be the messenger of bad news. I'm just an economic storm reporter.

Remember, this story is not written in stone yet. It's a gray area. We have the power to create our future outcome in some ways. Let's become the spiritual miracles that we are, and we can escape the worse of this banking and political breakdown. The main reason I wrote this book is because I love humanity, all creatures, and plant life. Now, I must pass this mantle to the next explorer to cut a new path. This chapter of my life is closing. This little crisis has slung me around like a rag doll for years. Someone else will have to carry the economic torch of light now. I'm done!

A Relapse of the Collapse

I guess I had to write about the actual breakdown of the global financial system. Understand this. I am not a fatalist. I am by nature an optimist. I really don't want to write this next chapter, but some fierce financial forces are approaching us at a rapid rate so I guess this is my calling. I hope I'm wrong on this call. It may be time for everybody to think the unthinkable. I've been thinking and living the unthinkable for years now. All of you will be contemplating the incomprehensible visions soon. Probably one of the most disturbing themes in this entire hullabaloo is that most collapses seem to happen because of an ignorant public following even more mindless leaders.

Hey, we are all ignorant but only on different subjects. It's totally normal to be ignorant about some topics. Who is it that claims to know the all of everything besides some politicians? No one walking around this planet can profess this declaration of title. Certainly not any of the present-day so-called leadership. Now, after the unprovoked military and financial bombs are blowing up all over the world from the Bush administration and Wall Street madness, only a fool would not be able to recognize the danger that we are in today. Now the entire economic system is operating on the level of an old-time jalopy with nothing left in the tank.

The stock market currently has been reduced to nothing more than an infomercial for suckers. The TV pundits are trying to sell you their goods just as though you were watching the jewelry channel. That is why it is of absolute significance that the influential government supervisors must carry on with the intentions of guiding this country's destiny to safe and sound grounds. It is true that a nation from time to time can act like a school of fish in the ocean. If the school of fish always trusts their leader fish to point them in the right direction, they sometimes will relax. Then they can be lured into taking the wrong turn. The leader fish can betray them and they all end up in the mouth of a giant predator fish. As I said before, "Before Wall Street died, they ate us alive."

When I reflect back on this thriller, several thoughts come to mind. Well, one of my first references that I zoomed in on in trying to determine if this is the moment of truth is this. In the year 2007, the credit crunch ripped the economic systems of borrowing and lending to pieces. As a matter of fact, as I have stated in the beginning of this book, many in the financial know thought for sure that the entire economic collapse was imminent. There was little chance of stopping a total financial failure by the fall of 2008. Then the bailout bonanza came about, and the loot and scoot was in full effect mode. Not only did the bailouts and the so-called stimulus packages delay the day of reckoning, but the Fed gang along with Wall Street decided to kick the bucket down the road—a technique also known as delayed devastation.

In other words, not on the Bush watch. If the enforcers of the rules of the financial industry had applied the law on the books, then so many of Wall Street's and the White House's erroneous plans from the years from 2000 to 2008 could not have been activated. So they panicked and made several mistakes. The regulators would do anything so long as the collapse did not manifest itself during Bush's final year. In reality though, the collapse did happen during the Bush administration's term in office. Bush Co. just could not bring themselves to be perceived as the ones who were in charge while the greatest financial blowup in this nation's history and the world happened. If you were paying attention, that's exactly what happened. There were those who were watching the collapse happen and those who were copping some Z's when they were supposed to be guarding the monetary henhouse.

Now, you must understand that a breakdown of an economic system of this size does not just happen in a short period of time. I've heard the many theories about the history of the financial failures which began when the Fed was created. Also, I've heard about the history of theories explaining that this is the reason why, and that is the reason as to why we are in this mess. I really get it that it's an entanglement of past, present, and future economic commitments. I'm just writing about what I saw in the years of 2007 and beyond. I know the U.S. free market capital system blew up during this time. Many others saw this, too. It wasn't just these years that the slamdown happened. The economic information from the years leading up to this disaster is easy to find on the Internet. Just do some reverse engineering on the subject, and you'll come across some of the reasons as to why we are where we are. During these years I thought for sure that this was it for the global financial system! I was walking around with a deep pit of gloom in my body system.

Then the extend-and-pretend propaganda machine went into action. The game was, "At all costs, just don't let this economic breakup show up on our watch!" The Bush administration's Treasury Department and other fiscal agencies kicked that bucket of collapse crap so far down the road that the bucket was only barely recognizable anymore. So is the economy unrecognizable at this stage. As a matter of fact, they just destroyed that bucket and kicked it over the cliff, never to be seen again in its former shape.

Hide the evidence. Most of these bucket kickers did know the fake Jake strategy plan of "Not on my watch." Some lessers didn't really know why they had to kick that bucket. They were already worn out from kicking so many other buckets down the road. Start with the buckets full of the 9/11 truth seekers, the war invasions of the Middle East, the Hurricane Katrina disaster, the Wall Street sneak attack, the torture allegations, the NSA illegal spying, and a host of other buckets that did a swan dive off of that cliff. Instead of calling it the White House, they should have called it the Bucket House. Maybe we should call Obama "Super Bucket Man!" Able to stand on a bucket and leap over the truth in a single bound. The mass stream media was happy to assist the bucket kickers by covering up this political sportsman's event.

By the media missing the economic calls, they have helped to cover up the different stages of these monetary cocktails. I wrote in this book about the credit crunch of 2007, the market crash of 2008, the recession of 2009 that began in December 2007 to the spring of 2010, and finally I'm writing about the collapse of the summer or fall of 2011. If you missed the earlier blowups, I'm sure you won't miss the collapse. It will be news that is reported worldwide, maybe. Who am I kidding? None of the rest of the phases was big news at the time they were happening. Let's hope this last one don't catch the public by surprise. This just ain't about Wall Street anymore. Now it's about World Street. A humanitarian mission to save the species.

Now, at this date of May 4, 2010, this economic event is not on its last leg. This commotion looks like a centipede that has a hundred legs with at least ninety legs still to come down on the people. The whole hullabaloo has quieted down to a whisper. There are no more buckets to kick. Once again, the Federal Reserve has used up its ammo. I witnessed the Fed throw trillions of dollars trying to save the market in 2008 to 2010. The investors couldn't care less. There are no more stimulus plans that are coming to the rescue. The U.S. government has to be running out of funds because they are funded by the very public tax dollars that are disappearing like thieves in the night. No money creates no funny.

In other words, "Our time is up." We can no longer afford to spend more than what we have as a nation. To afford any debt outside of your means to repay the debt as a government will not be the new normal. This is a pot of dollars at the end of the rainbow that is losing its value fast. Remember the motto from the Popeye cartoon character Whimpy, who says "I'll gladly pay you tomorrow for a hamburger today." This forward debt lending process will never exist again as the model it once was. You will have to pay for that burger when it's ready, or you won't be eating today! Those days of pretend-and-lend are over.

We as a people must become better informed about these matters and realize we are in historic times. Our very existence is at risk. When these organizations run out of funds, so do we. All of the layoffs, unemployed and underemployed citizens not paying into the government coffers will disturb the health of all the world's wealth. Remember the American consumer is the number one driver of the national and global economies. Without America, there is no money show to be seen anywhere on the planet!

Final Straw

Since I became involved with chasing this stock market failure, I always wondered just how the final straw would present itself. Would something in the U.S. just blow the roof off of the banking system? There are many ways to speculate on this topic, but lately the picture of how the finality of the financial system may occur is becoming clearer into focus. Now, I must admit that I have been waiting for the next terminal shoe to drop on American finance for some time now. I just figured that the government and banking slicksters could not keep holding their bag of tricks together for too much longer. Something had to give. But the tap dance went on unnoticed by most.

Then on Thursday, May 6, 2010, one of the most dramatic days ever in the stock market's history happened. The Dow Jones crashed a thousand points within a thirty-minute timeframe. Now, I've already written in an earlier chapter that if the Dow Jones ever lost a thousand points at this stage of the weak market gains, it's time to run for the stock market exits. To my amazement, it happened! The stock market tanked that ominous day not long ago. As I stated in the beginning of this book, the world got scared on May 6, 2010, and the world didn't know it.

This was nothing less than the shot across the bow! I've been expecting this aftereffect of the financial system default for some time now, but it still caught me by surprise. Whenever a shift of this epic significance stirs, it's just really hard to accept. That thousand point drop-off was the final cough of the stock market cadaver's last breath, in this author's opinion. I know the economic media's circus tricks are saying that the Dow Jones shocker was maybe some trader with a so-called fat finger mistake, but I perceive this slamdown as the stock market giving its participants the fat finger! You know, the old "Up yours, too!"

These are prophetic times we are in. The weekend after the thousand point drop-off is here. Wall Street and the White House are nervous as can be, not knowing just what the opening Monday on the stock market will present investors and traders with.

My knees were shaking, also. By Sunday the 9th of May 2010, I personally declared that day to be Black Sunday. There are no fundamentals operating in the market. You can't build a house on quicksand. Now investigations are checking into just what caused that thousand-point ambush. They say a computer glitch could be the culprit. Who knows if anyone will ever find out? In the meantime, don't just toss my theory out to the curb. There could be something to it.

So in the end, we may have an actual 2010 relapse of the first 2008 collapse. They refused to let the first collapse proceed, so we are now in a relapse. I know this may be confusing to you, but believe me when I tell you this; it's also made scrambled eggs out of my logic, too. Maybe by compromising with our debt problems the first time around, we created this blowup that we have today. It seems it would have been wiser and less costly, judging by the riots in Greece and austerity plans of today to get it right the first time. Now we all may have hell to pay because a bunch of nitwits who did not want to deal with the original economic eruptions back then. Anything to save their skins and burn our bank accounts.

Now for all the folks who disapproved of the fact that somebody who held the office of the President was in charge of the nation when this crackup happened can't deny this anymore. Perhaps no one was in charge, which is my thesis throughout this book. You can call it a ghostly corroboration or a spooky financial intervention of misfits. Call it whatever you want to call it. Now is not the time for sleepwalking and talking. It ain't just about the lip city from the train of Hallelujah frontmen and women anymore. It's about action.

My friends, I don't know quite how to put these thoughts down in words. In this author's opinion, we have reached the final threshold. We will need an economic miracle just to maintain any resemblance of our current lifestyles. I am not responsible for the crashing of the premier free market capitalistic system. I'm just a guy who happened to peep in on some financial bones of contention going down. I'm only scribbling some of my thoughts down on paper. Many other merry men and merry women were right there in the master funding mix when it was blowing up on their watch. They have taken us to the brink. We are at the point of no return if something does not change quick, fast, and in a hurry. Sorry to be the messenger of this troubling news. Remember, don't kill the messenger. If we should happen to make it through these Earthly trials, may we never be deceived so easily again by oath-taking government employees, nor impressive bankers or lawyer types.

All the financial experts that I trust are screaming for people to get on the sidelines today. Don't go long in this stock market. Take your 401(k)s and pension plans and convert them into hard cash. At least for the short term, the dollar is becoming a safer bet than the euro. Get into cash. Like I said, buy the supplies you'll need for your family. I've always believed "It's better to break your heart, than let you be destroyed." I'm not sure that everything in this book is correct. I tried to do the best I could with an overwhelming event. It's a dirty job, but somebody had to do it. Lastly, I'm throwing my lucky penny in the wishing well of hope and making a wish for the continuation of the species of all living creatures and things as the Creator meant them to be so. A matter a million times true. Keep your head up from your neck up!

Goddess Sophia, please bless America and the world, so mote it be.

European Downfall

Just lately, Greece and the European Union are entangled in an enormous financial web of economic confusion. You should really check into this! A financial firestorm has been lit in the EU and no one seems to know how to put it out. I have been wracking my brains to try and come up with a solution to these problems and I'm still drawing a blank. The Eurozone problems are so discerning that I don't know if I could do these issues any justice in explaining them, but here goes my best shot at it.

Back in the year 2001, the European Union accepted Greece as a Sovereign Nation State of the EU. From my understanding, the EU is a monetary organization and not a fiscal policy bureaucracy. In other words, the EU members all used the same currency, the Euro, but had no mobilized fiscal oversight that could be triggered on behalf of the EU for financial protection of the union. Each nation was to perform strict fiscal and monetary policy on their own. Yeah, right! You know that is not going to work with rogue politicians and bankers in these countries involved. So much for the One World Order mission. Hell, you can't even get One Union Order. I've often wondered who has the most efficient financial system, Europe or America. I have already described some of the EU's policies. I'm guessing that you are already aware of the U.S. economic system habits, the one where the Federal Reserve calls a lot of the monetary and fiscal shots, but the organization operates with no serious oversight of their financial commitments on the country's behalf. In other words, they operate outside of the Constitutional law of this nation. Which system of commerce would you prefer? Door number one or door number two? They are both obviously inadequate schemes for nations of this size. They both have failed miserably.

OK! Enough of that stuff again. Now back to Greece. Now, to qualify to become a member of the EU, your debt-to-GDP ratio had to be less than 3%. Greece at that time seemed to check out and pass muster. Well, to speed the story fast forward moving up to the year 2010, Greek politicians and banking interest had lied about their financial stability and instead of the 3% curve, the Greeks had more of a deficit than had been exposed. Their debt-to-GDP ratio was at 14%. Now a chain reaction in relationship to the Greece debt has been activated in Europe. Because of the problems in Greece, traders and investors don't believe that the debt conditions can be met in a proper timeframe.

Let the bailouts begin. Germany is the largest player in this whole governing body of the EU. When this fiasco first erupted in the early spring of 2010, the German citizens refused to bail out Greece. Now they have no choice but to bail them out or else they will go down in flames with Greece, the entire European Union, and the world, for that matter. That sucks. Then, there's the moral hazard of once you bail out Greece, where does it stop" That's what the Germans are really concerned about. When do the stimulus plans end? Maybe never. That's the Catch 22 for the Germans. Damned if they do and damned if they don't. They could be throwing their hard-earned wages down the Eurozone's black hole for many years to come. Just like the Americans. Good money after bad money. I can understand their reluctance to being a party to a bailout for the EU because their funds will be the main banker of last resort for the European Union. They are saying "Screw you, Greece." Sadly, they may say these words, but they will have no choice but to rescue their Greek brethren whether they want to or not. Checkmate! Sometimes life just ain't fair. By the way, Greece is in hot water with another large payment that's due around May 20, 2010. They have no way to pay for it.

Then Greece got downgraded by the rating agencies. That added more wood to the fire. Next, the flames spread over to Portugal, then Spain, Ireland, and Italy. All of these nations may need a bailout now. Greece is a small country compared to Spain's total GDP of the Eurozone. Spain is the fourth largest in Europe. Their GDP is twice as large as Greece, Ireland, and Portugal combined. What certainty do the Germans have that bailing out Greece is the solution to fixing their problems? Who knows? What I do know is that the investors and traders are not waiting around to find out. They have effectively shut Greece down. The riots are getting more intense every day. Greece is only one country to keep your eyes on in the Eurozone.

Wow, you see what I mean as far as looking for an answer to this puzzlement of disastrous policies. One of the craziest sideshows in the complete debacle is the assistance from the International Monetary Fund bank. This bank's funds are basically supplied using American taxpayer-led legal tender contributor or money to bail out the Eurozone. The IMF is only allowed to bail out nations. So, California and New York suck it up. Sure, other countries contribute to the IMF's coffers, but the American banks at around 18% are the largest donors. The Americanos are being served again.

The European impact was so severely affecting the markets that the contagion of the Eurozone had caught most experts by surprise. During the coming week of May 10th through the 14th, I had also declared the whole week to be a return to the economic Dark Ages. I was feeling that we had arrived on the doorstep of doom. There was no way out. The global financial system was in serious trouble. Neither the EU or the euro would survive. Then to the rescue came the Federal Reserve of the U.S., Canada, the Swiss, England, and others came charging into Europe, swords raised and sliced out an unprecedented trillion-dollar bailout for the purposes of assisting in Europe's financial difficulties. The U.S. Fed opened up the TARP program and made American taxpayer funds available to bail out Europe when we can't even bail out the school music programs of America.

Now, this whole scheme to save Europe is not going to work using our taxes to save the EU. Here's why I say this. The euro is losing its value fast. Now, all sixteen nations of the Eurozone use this currency that is deflating rapidly. That gives these European banks little room to wiggle because their currency, the euro, is becoming worthless. That's a lot of nations to support for Americans along with Iraq, Afghanistan and many others. The TARP program was only revised recently because of the emergencies that the European banking calamity was exposing. Now, can you believe that the door to the American bank accounts is supposed to support the entire sixteen nations of the Eurozone. So, the greenbacks are the only things that are between the euro and the Eurozone going the way of the dinosaurs. That's a blowmind all by itself! In other words, if America does not create a constant flow of currency in the form of dollars to lend to the European Union banking system, the game is over. Europe has an investor credibility problem along with an insolvency crunch. Anyone with half a brain knows this TARP lending program of U.S. taxpayer funds can't go on forever. Hold on and fasten your economic crash seatbelts.

Yes, I am disclosing that the European Union wild card took me somewhat by surprise. There's only so much one man can keep up with. As I mentioned before, I have no research team to help me. So as Rome burns, so too may the rest of the world. Once Europe goes up in flames, this will certainly be a flash point for the rest of the world. It won't be long before the entire world flares up to ignite a glowing inferno of worthless paper currencies. Many of the banks will freeze up and stop lending. Even right now, Greek banks are having a hard time receiving investment funds into their accounts. They are not allowed to be an active participant in the global money system. Everyone expects America to be doing the same debt dance that the EU is doing very soon. Like I asked before, Ain't Deleveraging Fun? NOT!

The European Union is headed for a default! That's the simple fact of it. No one can stop it. This is really scary stuff. You see, America and the world cannot make it without the EU doing well. This is Europe I'm writing about. A big 'Mamma Jamma'! Germany is also involved in this mix. There are other countries besides Greece whose butts are in the frying pan. Try Portugal, Ireland, Italy, Spain. All the so-called PIIGS Nations are standing on compromised ground today as I write this chapter. We could all be riding in the big punishing parade if no one figures out how to get this EU quandary under control. This is absolutely urgent … or else!

The system of economic exchange is not going to wait for us to pay attention to the moment before it breaks down. It's moving at an accelerated speed right now, even as you read this book. In the years 2007 to 2010, the financial model was about a bailout of the banks. The current times find that the shift is now about humanity bailing out on the system. Now the whole episode has become downright dull for me. I refuse to listen to anyone telling me about how the stock market is operating in its current state. This is an old story for me now, years later. When you have been falling down the rabbit hole of collapse at a brisk drop rate for as long as I have, you get an instinct for where the financial bodies are buried in this market.

This very day, November 2, 2009, my wife and I are discussing relocation plans out of California. You gotta do what you gotta do in this economic jungle when trying to stay ahead of a paradise of irrevocable suffering. Everyone is going to be doing something when these changes happen… as you're doing now in your lives with historic economic changes going down daily. Hey, I don't have every answer, but I do have some qualified presumptions as to where this will all end up. Well, the fundamentals in the stock market are so far nowhere to be found. A nation cannot be a successful free-market capital system without a healthy banking system. What is capitalism except the flow of commerce, legal tender throughout the banking syndicates' offices of data? When the credit crunch froze the credit lines, making it harder to get a loan for a house or anything else for that matter, the size of the banking problems grew from many ugly infants to a village of despised giants.

You know that it's getting down to the nitty-gritty time whenever the phrase Plan B is spoken. It's true in this case also. This is the accumulation of my entire journey encapsulated in these next few statements. Making the call is the whole point. I didn't do all of this research to be wrong. Even my email address from five years ago is a sign for me: rjshoutout@yahoo.com. Is that just a coincidence or not? What call am I talking about, you might ask? The phase of a time shift where I will activate my Plan B or alternative scheme of existence. The time when you must decide that it's not about profits, but about preserving what resources you have. I recall the time when Wall Street investors left the building in 2007-08. They became less concerned about their profit margins and more concerned about holding onto their asses. They bolted out of the high profits and risk markets into lower risk investments.

Make no mistake about it. This is a traders' market. The TV pundits can speak about this being an investors market until the pigs fly. That's just not the facts, and has not been for years. Since the summer of 2007 when the credit crunch happened, this has been an extremely high-risk market for only the slickest of traders or hedge fund sharks. Most others would be advised to stay out of the shark-infested Wall Street waters. There can be any number of outcomes from this dollar blowup. Only you can decide your strategy for improving your chances to witness the New Age in peace, something that I wish we all will experience. According to the Mayan visions, the climax of this transformation triumph will peak on the date December 21, 2012.

May the God of your heart always shine its light of consciousness upon you and give you peace.

Many blessings,

Renard

ABOUT THE AUTHOR

Renard, also known as RJ, worked as a children's television personality in the San Francisco Bay Area for thirteen years. He and his wife Lori hosted a block of cartoons on KTVU Fox Channel 2 and Warner Bros. WB 20. He has been involved in projects to assist the atypical child for many years. Renard, Lori, who is a musical director for a school of special needs children, and therapist Shanti Malladi OTR/L, created a CD project titled "Social Skills the Musical Way" in 2002 to assist in the development of the kids. It is available at SouthPawEnterprises.com.

A native of Shreveport, Louisiana, who attended the Southern University jazz program, Renard has traveled the world while performing in R&B funk bands as a bass player and vocalist. He currently lives in the Bay Area, where he and his wife perform in Cotton Candy Express Music, a musical duo. He also performs in an adult band called Groovolution. Along with enjoying talking to his family, sports, and power walking at the ocean, he is currently writing two new books. The first is titled *The Great Light Experiment of Humanity,* and the second one is titled *Fukushima Daiichi: My First One Hundred Days of Hell.*

Renard is a concerned citizen who became an economic investigator when he noticed a flawed budgetary undercurrent in 2006 that was not working in the public's favor. This was the story of his journey down "Weird Street" and beyond.

www.ingramcontent.com/pod-product-compliance
Lightning Source LLC
Chambersburg PA
CBHW030005290326
41934CB00005B/233